# SUSAN MEISELAS
## ON THE FRONTLINE

# SUSAN MEISELAS

EDITED WITH MARK HOLBORN

# ON THE FRONTLINE

Thames & Hudson

Pages 2–5: Clothing, unearthed in the search for identification of those buried anonymously, marks graves, Arbil cemetery, Northern Iraq, December 1991
Pages 6–7: Villagers watch the uncovering of a mass grave in Koreme, Northern Iraq, 1992
Pages 8–9: Dr Clyde Snow, internationally known forensic anthropologist, holds the blindfolded skull of an executed male teenager estimated to be between 15 and 18 years old, Arbil, Northern Iraq, 1991

# 1
## THE EXCHANGE

# 44 IRVING STREET

From the outset, the idea of a narrative that extended beyond the single frame lay at the heart of my work. I can love certain photographs that I have made, but that is often not quite enough for me. The making of an image and the image itself don't always hold me long enough. Despite the pleasure of making a photograph, I still feel the need to stitch it and weave it into something more. I want to know what the subject says, beyond what the picture shows. I want to explore how the viewer can be invited into the exchange. The photographs are immediate personal encounters that last only a moment. These encounters may later create a bridge for constructing larger narratives, which go beyond someone's personal story to a wider national or cultural history. The picture is then merely the starting point.

I didn't formally study photography through college. My stronger visual education was through cinema. I was captivated by the immersive documentary experience of Frederick Wiseman's *Titicut Follies*, his 1967 film on patient inmates of the Bridgewater State Hospital in Massachusetts. The very edgy, discomforting questioning of the voyeuristic aspect was immensely powerful. It made a greater impression on me than the *New Documents* show at the Museum of Modern Art that same year, which included the work of Diane Arbus, Lee Friedlander and Garry Winogrand. I wanted to be engaged through photography. I looked at it, I enjoyed it, but I couldn't see myself working as a street photographer.

In 1968 and 1969 I travelled around the world on an International Honors Program and used a camera, but it was still only an exploration and not yet part of my identity. In the fall of 1970 I joined a Masters course in Visual Education at Harvard. I learned a lot about making photographs in three months, but I still didn't identify with the idea of becoming a photographer. I remember the awkwardness rather than the pleasure of working during that period.

Self-portrait, 44 Irving Street, Cambridge, Massachusetts, 1971

44 Irving Street was the house in which I lived, and it provided me with a framework for a photographic project for the first time. I was looking at people who were strangers, yet my neighbours. I didn't know them, even though I lived among them. We were each separated in our own spaces. Having seen August Sander's portraits, maybe I saw evidence of a kind of typology. I was not going beyond my front door to work. There was no need to travel, but I did have to knock on closed doors.

I had a camera, a 4 × 5, which was very visible, yet I was hidden under a black cloth behind it. In the restricted space of a small room, the camera stood in for me. I had to confront the idea of who I was. I was also intruding, which is a very big first step. It felt like trespassing. To make a good portrait, you need to reveal a private moment, which can feel like an act of theft. Then there is both the possibility of the construction of the portrait and the capture of a moment. I wanted to place myself in the boarding house because I lived there and was present. At the same time I felt invisible. That invisibility creates a tension throughout my work. I am present, but want to avoid the focus on myself. I am not a 'fly on the wall': I don't pretend not to be there, but I am not the 'story'. I might be the bridge, the guide, and in some sense the collaborator with the subject.

I first showed the Irving Street portraits to the subjects and asked them how they saw themselves in my photographs. When we had a small show of the work, I hung their written notes next to the photographs. I was experimenting with how to bring their voice into the work. The subject has to want me to be there for me to feel that I can be there. This was the central space of collaboration, along with an act of reciprocation, that I was trying to discover right from the beginning.

Ellen, 44 Irving Street, Cambridge, Massachusetts, 1971

# CARNIVAL STRIPPERS

In the summer of 1972, my partner Dick Rogers and I took a road trip across the country to photograph small circuses and state fairs. That was how I first found the carnival strippers. I wasn't looking *for* them. At first I was just looking *at* them, like everyone else. I was trying, from the outside, to make sense of what was going on from the perspective of the fairgrounds. I mostly was watching people gawking. By the second summer, when I returned, the manager recognized me and knew that I was intrigued and wanted to meet the women. A return always offers a new possibility. There was that feeling: 'You've remembered me.' So, the door opened a little more. I felt I had to go much further than the fairgrounds view alone. I had to get inside.

First I was invited into the dressing room and sat through the long nights of the women coming and going to perform, either dancing on the front bally, which faced the fairgrounds and the general public, or stripping on the back stage, which was under a separate tent accessible only to men. At some point, one of the women pulled the curtain aside, saying, 'There they are.' I could not imagine what going out on stage was like. They were leading me to look. They talked about the empowering experience of literally being above the men and having them in the palm of their hand.

There were two ways of photographing that interaction: either through the curtain of the dressing room, looking out at the back stage, or from within the tent, behind the men looking at the stage. The only way to capture the latter was to dress as a young man. The manager was fine as long as I wasn't revealed as a woman. Their famous call was 'No ladies, no babies'. If you look carefully at the contact sheets, very few of the male eyes were looking at me. They were gazing at the show. I was working with one small Leica and in some cases discreetly hand-holding long exposures. No flash. The act of looking was shared, but the spectators were as

The Star, Tunbridge, Vermont, 1975

central as the spectacle. Like the people on the fairgrounds and inside the tent, I was 'looking', and in making photographs I was also implicating the viewer in regarding the spectacle.

I started to audio-record all the exchanges: with the manager, amongst the women themselves, with the men who were hanging out or watching, and with the wives of the men. A little of this approach came from my limited ethnographic studies. I wanted to see the whole world of the carnival strippers from within, as well as looking out. At the centre of that world was the show. Feminists at that time perceived the girl shows as exploitative places and thought the women were victims. But I was more interested in seeing how they were seen within their world, and hearing what the women said about themselves rather than what other people said about them. I was drawn to know what motivated them. Partly, but not wholly, their reasons were economic. Yet they revealed other aspects of what it meant to be a woman and to have to use their body in that way. They were not in control, or not as much as they thought they were. They were on the edge where the tease tested them. They were pushing and asking, 'How far can I go?' These were not just nudes, but real women with personal histories.

There is always the challenge of access, but then the question, what are you doing here? What do you bring? What do you contribute, and for whom? As the fairs were moving from one town to another, I would go back to Boston, where I was based, and make contact sheets, which the women would mark up when I returned at the weekend. Portraits were almost always what they wanted to gift to others – their lovers or their fathers. The women chose which pictures they liked, though the choices were not necessarily those that later appeared in the published book. Most importantly they were seeing what I was seeing, and this was as fundamental as it was for my neighbours on Irving Street.

New girl, Tunbridge, Vermont, 1975
Pages 24–25: Before the show, Tunbridge, Vermont, 1974

Today people can show each other their digital screens or upload their pictures, but at that time film was very secretive. Shooting with film meant you had captured something of that other person – maybe another reason why the way that the great street photographers were working wasn't right for me. I needed to share what I had seen, to give it back.

In many cases, there is an exchange in which the presence of the photographer demands the acknowledgment of the subject. I could see how, say, Diane Arbus was working effectively with direct encounters, but that was exactly opposite to my comfort zone. I did not like my subjects looking at me; nor did I want the 'subject' to become an 'object'.

By 1975 I was teaching and trying to transcribe the two hundred hours of tape that I had recorded in order to make the book *Carnival Strippers*, which came out in the fall of 1976. There had been the possibility of making a film during that period, and Dick and I tried to raise the money. I still have our shooting proposal. Sadly we couldn't find the financing. This is where changes in digital technology have expanded opportunities, not least in terms of affordability and possibilities for visual narrative. If there had been small camcorders, then I am absolutely sure I would have made a film. Instead I tried to make a book that was somewhere between what a film could accomplish and conventional publishing, by interspersing photographs with excerpts from the recordings and thus giving voice to the subjects. The voices weren't telling a specific story behind a particular picture. The pictures and the text were parallel narratives: they didn't need to match, but together they created an environment. The voices bring you into the subjects' psychological space, just as I was trying through the pictures to bring you in to experience their working lives. I became progressively more comfortable being inside the world where I was photographing. I formed relationships with the women that led to travelling with them for weeks at a time. The relationships evolved. Even though I was invisible, the work was based on those relationships. They were getting to know me and I was getting to know them. I became immersed in their lives, and sustained connection to some of them through extensive letter exchanges on the off season to the travelling summer shows.

The first show of the work was at CEPA, an experimental gallery in Buffalo, New York. I made separate groupings of pictures, going from the outside fairgrounds to the dressing rooms and the back stage. Each series was installed in a different small space, and each had floating sound with a mix of voices. It was the most perfect representation of the work.

I don't see myself as an artist just working within a community of artists. I am most interested in the community from which the work actually comes. I resist the cultural label of 'photojournalism', which puts one's work into a box. This work was not assigned or produced *for* a specific publication, but it was later seen *within* specific publications, and there lies a great distinction. It was first seen on walls, not printed pages. The women brought me in and the book later brought a hidden world to public attention, sharing a complex story from the inside out.

Pages 28–29: Backstage, Carlisle, Pennsylvania, 1975
Pages 30–31: Returning backstage, Essex Junction, Vermont, 1973
Pages 32–33: Between shows, Fryeburg, Maine, 1975

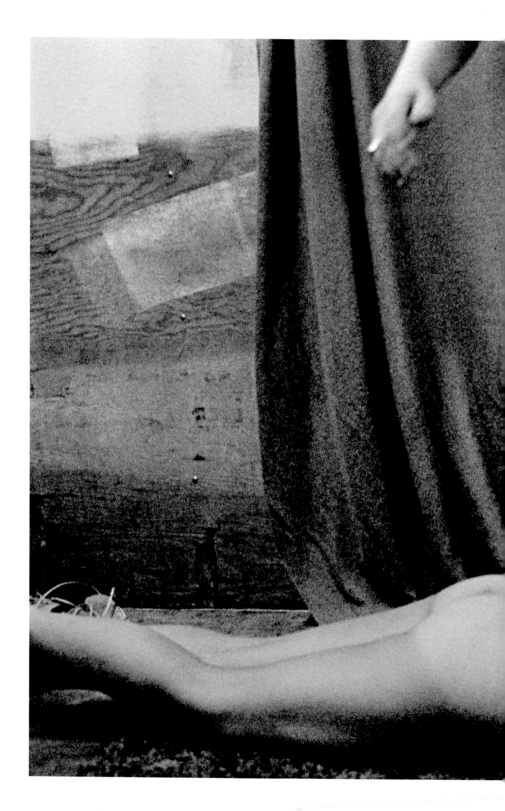

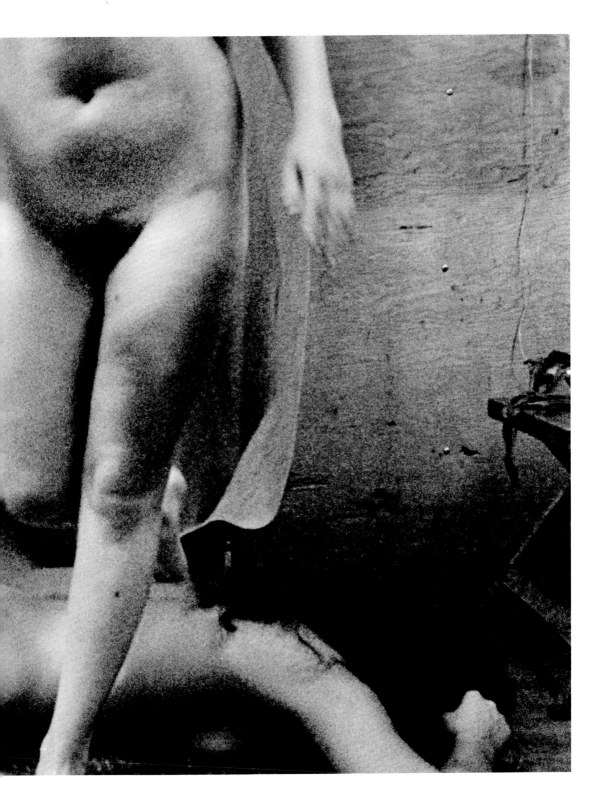

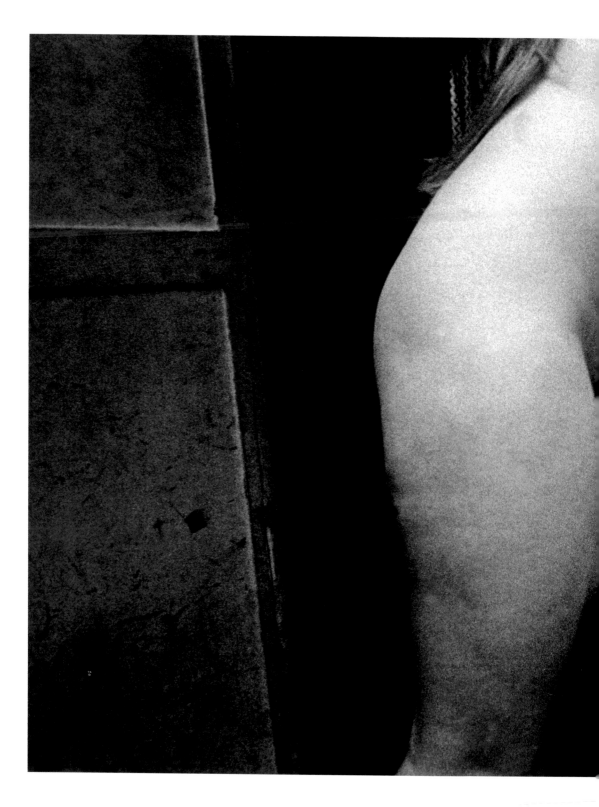

# PRINCE STREET GIRLS

I moved to Mott Street on the edge of Little Italy in 1974, and soon after met the girls who hung out on the corner of Prince. When I went out to the neighbourhood, I never knew what I would find or see. Leaving my front door and walking around, I had no plan. The girls might have been out on the street, or they might not. They might have been in the mood to have me around, or they might not. There was neither certainty nor intention, but slowly I began to observe these young girls on my block in the process of becoming women. They were posing and mimicking. In the early seventies there was little discussion about the dominance of a sexualized culture or the influence of advertising. So who were they imitating? Maybe they were posing to impress each other. The girls leaning on a pole were just being themselves. They were still in their awkward little bodies trying to find themselves.

I was fascinated by their relationships with each other. Some of them were related. They simply liked to hang out together. There was no story, no narrative. We didn't plan our encounters. I would be going out carrying my Leica and I'd see them on the corner, or there were moments when I met them with their mothers in the grocery store and made jokes about the girls coming to my loft, which was becoming their clubhouse.

The work was a subtle observation of puberty, but the process was ruptured just when they entered adolescence and I left the country. I had no idea then that I would be away for so long. When I returned, I only caught a few of their weddings. Since then they have all left the neighbourhood, though I still see them now and again when they ring my doorbell to show their daughters those early pictures.

The full story of young girls becoming women and going on with their lives, leaving the neighbourhood and having children, might have become a different, longer story. But I made a difficult choice to follow another path, and that had consequences.

Right: JoJo, Carol and Lisa, corner of Prince and Mott Street, Little Italy, 1976
Pages 36–37: Dee, JoJo, Frankie and Lisa after school on Prince Street, 1976
Pages 38–39: Pebbles and friend on the A train to Rockaway Beach, New York City, 1978
Page 40: Pebbles and JoJo on Baxter Street, Little Italy, 1978
Page 41: Pebbles, JoJo and Roe on Baxter Street, Little Italy, 1978

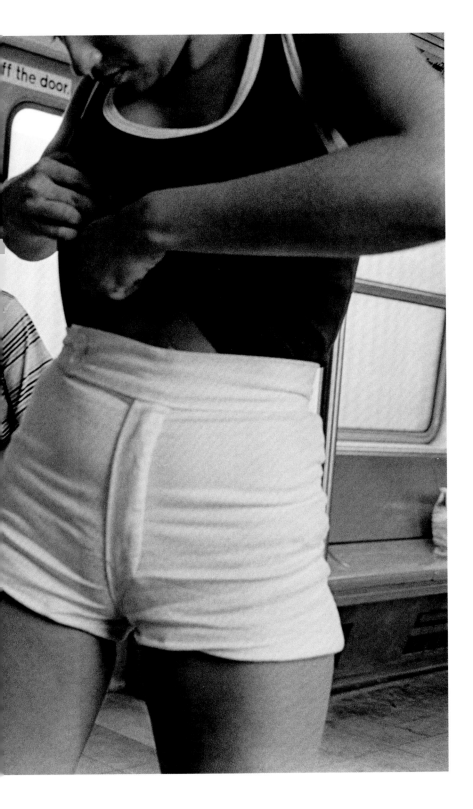

39

# PORCH PORTRAITS

During the early seventies I was teaching photography in primary schools in the South Bronx, New York. I was making pinhole cameras and using Polaroids with the kids, as part of an experiment in visual literacy, using pictures to tell stories that would become small books and hopefully inspire them to read their own words.

In 1975 I took an artist's residency to go to South Carolina and then Mississippi. Every afternoon after school I would take off alone. I would drive down a dirt road and see a little house. By then I had an excuse when I knocked on the door: 'I don't live here, but I am teaching at the local school.' The photograph of this house is still important to me. It's symbolic. I didn't know who was in the house or what was ahead. You have to trust that curiosity to drive down a road, and not know where it's going to lead you.

I was alone in these settings. There was no writer working with me to provide the context. No James Agee. It's just me and them. The photographs went nowhere except back to the people I photographed. I went home and printed and then posted them the picture, which felt like completing a circle. I would love to find one of those postcards in somebody's home one day to know if it was treasured or not. Again the question was: who is this work for? There is the gifting back in exchange for the giving of a moment of someone's time. There's a little signal that it's OK to be there and to look. It's a subtle communication. You catch it in their eyes or even in their lack of connection. It's just 'she's here' and 'we're here' and whatever is happening is happening. This is the opposite of the performance of a portrait. Is the woman in the doorway wondering what I'm doing? The girls on the steps are just hanging out, and I'm delighting in their gestures and their bodies. If we went back to the contact sheets we'd probably see a progression as they began to engage, and then they probably went back to the same play or games they were involved in when I first entered their view.

End of the road, South Carolina, 1974
Pages 44–45: Myra and friends, Greenville, South Carolina, 1974
Pages 46–49: Porter family, Lake City, South Carolina, 1974

# 2
## EL PUEBLO

# CUBA

I didn't anticipate that the publication of *Carnival Strippers* would lead to some surprising opportunities. In the spring of 1977, President Carter opened up limited travel to Cuba and I was invited to join a group of seven photographers travelling with the Center for Cuban Studies, which sponsored cultural exchanges.

The trip to Cuba offered a different way of working. I was in a place where I knew no one. I didn't speak the language. I didn't see most of the other photographers because we were all in small groups and on separate paths. A car was provided. We were driven to places from which we wandered. The Cubans took us everywhere, to a school for the arts, factories, medical centres and neighbourhoods. We were welcomed. I was fascinated by the creation of an alternative society that aspired to build on collective values. I was roaming the streets knowing there was nothing specific I had to make a picture of. While the aesthetic composition of a frame was as important to me as its context, there was just the pleasure of discovering and framing a moment.

This freedom also marked the end of a period of no obligation. History eventually compels you to act. I was approaching a decade of work in Latin America, and a state of constant transition. Beginning with Nicaragua, staying there, moving to El Salvador, returning to Nicaragua, going to Colombia, Chile and Argentina, and trying to understand the enormity of the events and the terror of those times.

Right & pages 54–57: Havana, Cuba, 1977

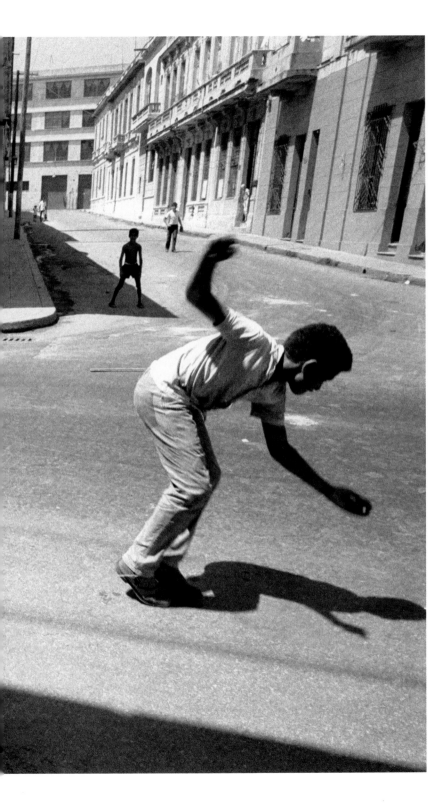

# NICARAGUA

I live two blocks from the Bowery, near the Volunteers of America, and between Thanksgiving and Christmas 1977 had begun following the men from the homeless shelter. At the time they were dressing as Santa Claus to go out to ring the bell on Fifth Avenue and gather money for the Volunteers. I imagined a narrative beginning with the fantasy of transformation – becoming a Santa Claus and ending up living back on the street. But I couldn't go into the homeless shelters like I could the motels with the strippers, and as I photographed the men it was hard for me to look at or hear about those broken lives. At the end of the season, when their role was over, I would sometimes find them passed out and drunk on my doorstep. I then followed them to a women's prison upstate, where some of the men from the Bowery were scraped up and dumped for detox. I imagined a cycle but couldn't complete it.

I was just starting to go out and discover the world through making pictures. I was exploring on my own, without writers. In contrast to the darkness of those whose lives were ending alone and in despair, I found Nicaragua compelling as a counterpoint because there was a society mobilizing to defeat a dictator. The only way to find out more was to pack up and go there.

When I read about the assassination of Pedro Joaquín Chamorro, the editor of the Nicaraguan opposition newspaper *La Prensa*, in January 1978, I had no idea where Nicaragua was on the map. Little snippets of news appeared in the international press: Chamorro's death had become a spark for the popular insurrection. Students were taking over the universities and workers were closing the factories. I didn't have an assignment, or even a schedule for returning. I clearly remember landing in Managua filled with anxiety. I had no idea where I was going to go, or what I was about to do. I knew nobody and there was no one to greet me. I had to find a room and figure out what to do the next day and the next and the next. I started in

Right: Traditional mask used in the popular insurrection. Monimbo, Nicaragua, 1978

a small hostel. I didn't stay in a hotel because I had very little money. I had to learn to tolerate uncertainty and develop a degree of resilience.

Small events were happening around me but they seemed disconnected. I didn't understand what they were or what they might lead to. I was moving around Nicaragua capturing isolated moments, documenting a process that was evolving. I stayed five or six weeks on that first trip and was shooting both colour and black and white. Maybe I shot fifty rolls, but I didn't know what I had until I came back home for two weeks and processed the film and saw what *The New York Times* chose to publish.

At that time black and white film was mostly used for documentary work, but right from the beginning colour felt right. I couldn't see the place or the people without it. I wasn't intending to do something different; I was simply responding to what I saw. Kodachrome Daylight 64 was beautiful film to work with. The black and white pictures served like a sketchbook. On later trips I started to process the black and white in my hotel in order to see what I was doing, but then I sent the rest of the exposed film straight back to New York. There was a whole chain of people involved in getting my film couriered, processed and edited, which I could not have done without Magnum's network.

In August the National Palace was taken by the Sandinistas and I immediately got on a plane. From then on I continued to go back and forth. The first offensive in August and September was crushed at the cost of several thousand, mostly civilian, casualties. By late fall I was trusted enough to have an encounter with an urban guerrilla cell. Though I was not blindfolded – that would have been too obvious – I was told not to look where I was going. I thought I could create a map in my head of all the turns left and right, but I could never retrace where I ended up. It was the middle of the night. At the place where I was taken, the young men were training to use guns.

After the first defeat the university and schools reopened. The rhythm of daily life was recovering, but many young people were going underground. Several months later I crossed the border into Nicaragua from Honduras and walked for ten days into the mountains. I was trying to understand the scale of their commitment from a different perspective.

During the last offensive the ABC journalist Bill Stewart walked out of a barricaded zone in Managua that had been taken over by the population and the Sandinistas. He was shot on the spot. His film crew documented the shooting. I had passed that very same barricade an hour earlier. His body was brought to the hotel where we were staying. Then the question of 'why him not me?' did arise. Somoza simply didn't want the world to know about the rebel movement. There were people who were killed in the crossfire, and then there were those who were specifically targeted.

After the National Palace was taken the world press had started to focus, but they never stayed very long. They would come and get what they needed, as if working with a checklist. I was applying a documentary process of staying with the events as they unfolded, and trying to capture the dynamics of what was taking place. The revolutionary triumph was in July 1979. The people had their revolution and after a couple of weeks I left to go home. By October there had been a coup in El Salvador that was to ignite an insurrection that lasted over a decade. I felt I had to be there. I was drawn to history, not to news.

Narration from *Voyages*, 1985,

co-written by Susan Meiselas and the filmmaker Marc Karlin

[**MK**] *'Maybe,' she wrote to us, 'it would be as well to begin at the end. If I'm going to write to you as your map-reader, and if I'm to answer some of your questions, let's begin at the end.'*

[**SM**] When the Nicaraguans, after a long separation, came together with shared hopes and a past on which they hoped they would be able to base a future, it was the ending of a period of struggle, which had left 50,000 dead, cities totally devastated and an economy in ruins. There was no time to celebrate, there was no fiesta. By the end of that day of July the 19th [1979], I was totally confused as to what my role was going to be. I had spent such a long time voyaging, getting close, being there and being with them, and in the process of that journey I'd come to realize that I was slowly losing my own country and beginning to feel that I had found a new one, only to find that suddenly on that day, July the 19th, it was their victory, not mine. I have pictures, they have a revolution.

It was the beginning of another kind of struggle, which was later to involve a painful and strange kind of separation. A lot of journalists were packing up again; the story as far as they were concerned was over. The InterContinental Hotel was filled with members of the international left wearing black and red scarves, colours that I could not wear even if I privately assumed them, as I am a professional, a journalist, a photographer. I photographed the clearing of the streets and wandered back to my room on my own. There's a call from my photographic agency: they suggest I come back home. Without any forethought I replied, 'I really don't have a home to come back to.' Bridging these two worlds and feeling pulled apart, that's when my photographs end. I begin to feel that these two worlds may not be reconcilable, that I may not be able to change sufficiently and fast enough to give up one for the other. So, as I said, it's just as well to begin at the end.

If you go to Nicaragua, like me you may cling onto images which are already pictures inside your own head. A collection of all the thousands of images you've already seen. You can't help it, despite your better instincts. You take images which drag you into taking them, and an inward anger results when you actually pull the trigger. I had left New York for Nicaragua not knowing what was going to happen, and knowing even less about Nicaragua. I had picked up *The New York Times* and had read an article on the death of Pedro Joaquín Chamorro, the editor of Nicaragua's only opposition newspaper. Central America then was not often in the news and if it had occasionally been reported, the reports had not lodged in my memory. What had driven me there was that I knew nothing about it, and yet the size and therefore the importance given to the article in *The New York Times* assumed that I should.

I remember somewhat painfully the early days of my journey, those early days of wandering around, drifting and feeling very unstructured. One day it was very hot; just to get up in the morning was an effort. I just drove around not even knowing what I was looking for. I was at the end of my patience; everyone else seemed to be rushing around doing what they had to do, and I felt aimless. I was in a downtown area, where people were living in rubble shelters, when I came across this woman who was washing clothes by a sewer. We stopped and we talked, and out came this man who was totally drunk. He was very thin and forthright, and was swearing that one day he would get Somoza. As this was the first time I'd ever heard anyone declare his open opposition to the regime, I felt frightened for his life and hoped that he would not say these things just to anyone. I felt protective: on the one hand, I was relieved at hearing someone say what he felt; on the other hand, I felt his vulnerability. He asked me to go back to his house with his wife, who was the washerwoman, and his children. His house was a pile of rubble. He asked me to sit down in a very authoritative manner. There was a semblance of a staircase, which led to an open sky, as there was no roof. He went upstairs and came back with a plastic bag wrapped up in rags. He carefully unfolded the rags and took out of the bag a gold bar. Pointing to it he said, 'That's what it's really like here. Believe it or not I found this, but I can't do anything with it, because if I went to a bank they would accuse me of having stolen it.' So he asked me if I could do anything with it. There it was, a gold bar, which had clearly come from a mine, and here he was with it. It could have changed his whole life, but there was nothing he could do about it. What was extraordinary about all this [...] – from having floated around for so long, having no connections, feeling strange, almost useless compared to the middle-class opposition who were organizing against the dictator Somoza, or to journalists who had definite set tasks, or to a resistance that I kept on hearing about but could not see – was suddenly to come close to someone in such peculiar circumstances. I never saw him again. Somoza cleared out the whole area that was full of refugees from the '72 earthquake. He was afraid that people would come crawling on their bellies through the weeds and reach his headquarters. He cut down all the weeds and got the squatters out of the area.

I spent most of my time walking around, trying to get familiar with the place; getting to know which quarters were the most militant by the amount of slogans that were written on the walls. I knew something was about to happen, and all my energy went into finding out what it was and where it was, but everything seemed secretive, unavailable, just tension and the heat. The tension could be seen, but photographed with difficulty. National Guard jeeps would rip around corners heading for destinations we dared not imagine. I remember asking people what was happening and being surprised how little they said, how quickly they would avert their eyes, which only much later on I became accustomed to. It was to do with who was listening and who could make use of what was said. As for me, I felt safe, extending the idea of the familiar, the expected, the I've-been-here-before feeling. Taking photographs which are safe to take because everybody has understood their role. I was an American, I had a passport, I was safe. I could travel, trespass, and I could leave. Photography seemed to be a perfect metaphor for this process; I could go from one point to another. Unlike the Nicaraguans, I was free.

I remember talking to another photographer after having been there just for two weeks. I said to him, 'Nothing's happened, I haven't done very much.' He told me to go out and just take pictures in the streets. 'But you don't understand,' I said. 'There is something happening. It's just that I can't see it, I can't get at it.' Value has always been placed on knowing, which I find has little to do with photography. But there is another kind of knowing, which is produced by sign-reading and knowing at another level. My involvement with Nicaragua really began with this picture [the body on the hillside, p. 66]. I found this place quite by accident. I'd heard about disappearances, but it was only after I had stumbled on it that I knew that it was really taking place. It was the first time I myself saw what I had so often heard whispered, hurriedly, in a bus queue or in a market.

*She went on to write that after two weeks she still felt as if she was a detective. She was still looking for something, not knowing where it was. She was still at the stage of knowing what you're looking for but not being able to find it. You've heard about it, that is, you've heard about the word 'repression'. But it remains hidden; it has no concrete manifestation and you can't photograph it. And so, stumbling on evidence, coming out of darkness, information through signs, having to learn a new language, was at the same time being continuously acknowledged and treated, as if she was an outsider. She tried to get rid of the notion that she had always been brought up with: namely, that everything should be constantly available, because there was little or nothing left to surprise one.*

Cuesta del Plomo, site of assassinations by the National Guard. Managua, Nicaragua, June 1978
Pages 68–69: Student demonstration broken up by the National Guard using tear gas. Managua, Nicaragua, June 1978
Pages 70–71: A funeral procession for assassinated student leaders. Demonstrators carry a photograph of Arlen Siu,
an FSLN guerrilla fighter killed in the mountains three years earlier. Jinotepe, Nicaragua, 1978

Behind each event lay an image that was never taken. Yesterday's newspapers never forecast what was going to happen next. No one could tell me things could happen, no one would tell me if they knew: the other side of being an American, a stranger, a potential enemy. So all I could do is to trace, anticipate and try to learn a new vocabulary. Suddenly, walking aimlessly, you would stumble on a fire burning, bonfires, one corner then another, broken glass, smoke and shouting slogans. Then the Guard would come: frantic scattering as gas tore through doors that had been slammed shut. Then there would be silence. Someone would grab me as guards on the outside shot, sprayed at the walls, at anything, for a bonfire, for nothing. Waiting, no one moved. To photograph or not, no aesthetic, just a decision to look out of the window. And so a picture with no power, no tension, not close enough. The experience is not in the image.

I always seemed to ride breathless in [...] at the end of events, just as they were finishing, adding emphasis and strength to the illusion that you could understand events without knowing why or from where they originated. You might say that's the condition of being a foreigner, not a journalist, whose professionalism should entail knowing. But we were living at a time when all there was to know remained deeply hidden. It was as if we were watching a mime whose intentions were clear enough but whose images I was unable to place.

Do you remember the green picture of the gas bomb [pp. 68–69]? I was outside the university and the paramilitary was slowly pumping live bullets into the campus. I stood outside, frozen, horrified, unable to go in, feeling distraught at being behind them. I decided to take the registration numbers of the paramilitary's cars and later give them to the students. It wasn't much, but I was beginning to trespass the bounds of simply being a journalist, an observer. It is worth repeating that it is always assumed that photographers know, but what we do not know is what scales were in – and then

No MÁS Asesinatos de
PARTE DE LOS Esbirro
y Tieles a la Dictadura

¡BASTA YA DE
REPRECIÓN!

LN

maybe fell from – our eyes. And so it has to be recognized that behind each picture there is a whole lot missing.

Within all that time, there seemed to be an air of normality punctuated by hurriedly written slogans on the walls demanding whether such-and-such a prisoner was still alive until suddenly, out of nowhere, would come the funerals. Eruptions, faces and slogans; again, private rituals, private ceremonies, not for the foreigner's gaze. There were too many missing histories. It's not only the fact that pictures are always going missing, it's a whole other time which to photograph obliterates. At a funeral procession where the mourners were carrying a portrait of Arlen Siu [pp. 70–71], I did not know then who she was. It was only much later on that I realized that she had been a guerrilla who had been killed three years earlier and it was only now that people were beginning to feel confident enough to be able to give her a funeral oration.

Slowly, I was beginning to understand: the problem with the photograph is that it always assumes that you've arrived, even before you've got there. So in the picture of the return from exile of the twelve representatives of the revolution, a loose coalition of middle-class interests opposed to Somoza, I could have represented them as leaders, but the question begged itself: for whom were they leaders? During this demonstration I became aware that there were no foreign correspondents present. They did not think that the political situation would be altered by this event: a judgment confirmed by the belief that if they are not present the event does not exist.

Having come to Nicaragua as a stranger, I found myself being asked to act as an image-maker. Some Indians from the town of Monimbo asked me to take a photograph of them practising throwing contact bombs in readiness for the coming insurrection. I was reluctant to take this picture, as I felt they were performing for the camera. I decided to take it [right] because so much of Nicaragua's history remained unknown

Right: Youths practise throwing contact bombs in forest surrounding Monimbo, Nicaragua, June 1978
Pages 74–75: Popular insurrection. Masaya, Nicaragua, September 1978
Pages 76–77: The fifth day of continuous bombing. Estelí, Nicaragua, September 1978

that I felt I had to respond to their demands to make *their* history visible. I went back to New York, and whilst there the photograph of the Monimbo Indians was used as the cover for *The New York Times Magazine*. This was the first photograph of the then-incipient Nicaraguan revolution to be published in an American newspaper. The fact that this was the last issue of *The New York Times* before it went on strike meant that the Monimbo Indians lay around doctors' waiting rooms longer than usual. That's how a single photograph can gain significance.

Suddenly, on that Sunday, the kids who, as it were, had been behind the slogans and the signs that I had seen in the previous voyage, erupted. The insurrection had begun. I had never seen people taking a risk before. There was a fascination for the kids with guns, but what qualified the fascination was the fact that their decision to take up arms could so easily end in death. If you see the kids first, and then you see them in relationship to airplanes and bombing, then their photographs take on a very different dimension. As it is, their photographs hide the choice and the risk that they took. I have been accused of photographing them as if they were in a fashion parade; it was them who chose by necessity to dress that way. Their fathers had probably given them a set of clothes which they wore underneath, so they could take off one layer and reappear without being recognized. Again, an example of photography's sad limits. The Nicaraguans would have understood, but as the photograph now faces you it is denied of its historical content, and it is the exotic fashion which seems immediately to justify it.

For the first time I'm aware of being forced in a professional kind of frame. I have to compete; I'm aware of tasks, deadlines, demands. I realize that I can only go in, shoot for two days, then I have to return to the capital to get the pictures sent back in order to meet the colour deadlines of American magazines. The beginnings of an ambivalence.

Fleeing the bombing. Estelí, Nicaragua, September 20, 1978

I remember being on top of a hill watching the bombing of Estelí and not being able to go inside. With me are a whole load of television crews sitting by their trucks drinking their beer. You have no idea what it was like standing outside, watching the bombing, and knowing what it must be like inside. I was overwhelmed; I was experiencing my own fears. I got sent by my agency a 400-millimetre lens because they felt I was getting too close to my subjects, which is how I'm able to take that picture of the airplanes bombing [pp. 76–77]. There is a lie in that picture, because it seems that I am very close; in fact, I'm miles removed from it, which is why I decide not to use that lens again, because I want to be close to what is happening.

To be close to the event is not sufficient to get rid of the contradictions. The dangers of being involved in this kind of professionalism [are] that you begin to fall short of the responsibilities involved when taking photographs of people who are in danger of losing their lives. In the picture I had taken of the kids with guns I make sure that I let the picture editor know that if he publishes these pictures he must choose only the ones where the fighters are masked. One morning, *Time* magazine, in which these pictures appeared, could be seen lying around the InterContinental Hotel, which was just opposite Somoza's headquarters. Some of the pictures published showed the kids unmasked. I rush back to Matagalpa, which by now is under siege, looking for the guys who were in the pictures. Not finding them I give them to a storekeeper, saying to him, 'Do you know who these kids are? I don't need to know, but make sure that they know these pictures exist.' That was the first time that I realized that a photograph could kill.

I think that most journalists think of photographers as mere illustrators of what *they* think. I don't agree; I did not trust what they thought particularly. You have to remember I was working with journalists who mostly knew each other. They had been together in Africa, Indochina, Asia. They had references they had brought with them; I was an outsider. All this accentuated the conflict I felt between, on the one hand, having to work like a professional photojournalist, and, on the other, wanting my photographs to be of some use to the Nicaraguans and their struggle. I was always conscious when taking photographs that I was trespassing on someone else's territory and then leaving again. I always felt the need to establish a dialogue between the photographer and her subject, always trying to give something back of what I had taken. But in this situation, amidst the bombing, the dead bodies and the grieving, there is no time to think of these questions. Half the time I am working in anger, at myself, at the situation. I can't believe what is happening. I am stunned at what people are having to go through. No time to think of past references, and the contradictions come pouring through.

Look at the woman: running away from the bombing with her baby [p. 79]. That photograph is taken by at least five different photographers, all at different points during her journey. She is literally vultured by us. No one is thinking to help her, including myself. We know now that photojournalism normalizes what are specific, and very violent, experiences, and we have thought around the subject ad infinitum, feeling guilty about photographs of terror becoming mere spectacle. We come up again and again against the same irritations, and we still find it impossible to do anything about it.

The people that are going up to the mountains are not guerrillas; they are mostly men who have had to leave their cities after the failure of the September insurrection, because the National Guard were arresting all young men between the ages of 12 and 25 as potential Sandinistas. I go to the mountains not because there is a possibility of a scoop or a magazine spread, but more in order to experience what the Nicaraguans are going through. Thousands and thousands went up to the mountains to take refuge.

Germán Pomares was there, an extraordinary man who spent twenty years fighting the dictatorship in the mountains. I remember being struck by his honesty and his open exchange with people. When food was ready, he would wait until everybody was served, and he saw to it that food was split equally. Afterwards, when night would fall, he would tell stories, recreate histories. He was deeply loved: he died [two months after I took his picture], bleeding to death because there weren't any bandages. My decision to go to the mountains is the closest I've got yet to being involved in their struggle without actually taking up a gun. They ask me if I would do so; I say no. They're puzzled by my constant snapping and recording until they ask me to take their photographs before they go on a mission in case they don't return. I have the strange feeling of people coming and going without any sense of the direction they're headed in.

I am still very much an observer. I'm learning a lot by putting together the pieces, and I remember going on top of a mountain and seeing all the little villages and towns around it and thought to myself, 'If I had been a Nicaraguan I wouldn't live down there, I'd be up in the mountains.' I begin to observe how much is not in the picture, such as the relationship between the city and the mountains and the feeling that in the city, where everyone has the potential of being an enemy, there is a lot that you can see but you can't photograph – such as underneath a mountain of corn: packages of medicine, guns. And then there's the kids delivering secret messages, a constant to-ing and fro-ing, and everywhere, the fear.

My passport, which had no Nicaraguan entry marked due to my being smuggled to the mountains from Honduras, made me realize for the first time that I could be arrested and seen as a participant. The line between the journalist and the participant gets vaguer by the moment. This time is also about attempting to establish relationships. In this atmosphere of shoot-outs, arrests, torture and executions I'm not easily trusted. The mistake that Somoza is making is that he's arresting people at random. Suddenly, everyone is vulnerable. But all around me I can see activities which are giving me greater confidence because it is obvious that the people are preparing.

When you're outside a process, as here you will often find yourself being, and you are not privy to their plans, it's hard to sustain your involvement if you don't understand what is happening. So you wait and wait. In the first voyage, when I asked people what's happening, they inevitably answered, 'They are coming.' They would shrug to each other or laugh to each other and repeat, 'They are coming.' 'Who are they?' No answer. When I asked this of women they would giggle to each other, as if my very presence as a foreigner was something that reassured them because they knew something that foreigners didn't.

When the first insurrection had failed, they knew it was going to be a harder struggle than they had anticipated. But finally, when the guerrillas did arrive down from the mountains, the myth that they represented was very important. You have to remember that the Nicaraguans did not know who their leaders were; they'd heard their names, they'd been told their stories and legends, but had never seen their faces. The same applied to their history because photographs of Sandino and his soldiers who had fought the Americans in the 1930s were censored out of all Nicaraguan history books.

By knowing who and where they were in the mountains I began to take photographs of the National Guard in a very different way than I had done before, because I was beginning to sense their end and their inevitable defeat. That is not what I feel about the paramilitary, who are arresting people in the streets and on the buses because they are totally outside the bounds of responsibility and law. The fear and anxiety that the paramilitary created was such that women would wait outside prisons hoping that their sons and husbands would be inside because it meant that they at least

Pages 84–85: Sandinistas in the mountains above Estelí, Nicaragua, April 1979
Pages 86–87: Search along the highway to León, Nicaragua, 1979

would have a chance of surviving. To the paramilitary it was simple: men, women and children who were not like them were an enemy, and therefore, to them, everyone was an enemy.

*In the final part of her letter, she wrote to us that up till then it had all been a process of trying to get closer, of trying to capture things as they were happening, so that slowly people behind the slogans and the signs would begin to appear. During all this time, she went on to write, she was being asked to act as an ambassador. 'Please, tell them what is happening.' The feeling that she had no power. 'I could take a photograph,' she wrote, 'but I have no control over where it would end up, how they would use it.' Your role as a free agent is being continuously circumscribed by being asked to do something for the revolution, not just for yourself.*

And now, the final insurrection. I keep on going back to Estelí because of my knowledge of what's above them in the mountains. My estimation of the uprising in Estelí is wrong, as a result of which I'm not in León when it is attacked by the Sandinistas. Estelí is finally under siege. They were experimenting with large slingshots to throw contact bombs, and they got a crop-duster plane to drop bombs near the headquarters of the National Guard. They built bonfires round which people banged tins to make sufficient noise to detract from the noise of the crop-duster planes. In Managua, nineteen districts were taken by the Sandinistas. They had worked it and planned it, and I had missed the barricade building and the organization behind it. I stayed there for two days. They don't see me particularly as a documenter, they still see me as an outsider, and it was very painful to me as I thought I had a very clear function. But they do not see me as such.

They're not sure whether they'll be able to hold the territory, so Managua is the only place where they're still wearing masks. As they could not take Managua, they had to escape at night to Masaya. During the final offensive they did not trust me, and in a sense quite rightly, because the professional side of me was coming to the fore. I'm now working for *Time* magazine on a guarantee; I'm like the others, I'm competing for the photographs. I feel a lot of anxiety about performing and yet at the same time I have a feeling for the sense of history that is evolving and escaping me. I was laden with images that I felt I had to get but could not get; it was a very chancy operation. If you're driving down the road you may come across it, it was not a matter of knowledge; the kind of knowledge I had was not useful. I think that the average journalist who would have been there for the length of time I had been might have covered it better because he would have responded simply to the news development rather than always trying to anticipate it. The professional, on the other hand, maybe would not have photographed people passing a cup of coffee: everyday moments do not make news.

I remember I was in New York when I learned that the final offensive would come soon. I wanted to get back as quickly as possible and I was trying to raise some commission money, but I was told in no uncertain terms that the pictures I had taken of the September insurrection would be just like the pictures of the coming offensive and that the newspapers could recycle them and use them again. After all, when you've seen one insurrection... I was outraged; I knew it could not be the same.

The young boy looking at the guerrillas [p. 91] reveals another sensibility at work and shows just how mystical the guerrillas were when they were in the mountains. As I said to you before, up till then it had all been a process of trying to get close and now I was as close to them as I could be. But however involved we are, the reality escapes you. We know we can always go back home. The Nicaraguans, of course, have nowhere else to go. It's more like playing for us; for them it's real, and that's an unbridgeable distance. We are protected by passports, white faces, cameras. And yet, there is always

Pages 90–91: One hour after the taking of San Isidro, Nicaragua, June 1979
Pages 92–93: Sandinistas at the walls of the National Guard headquarters:
'Molotov Man', Estelí, Nicaragua, July 16, 1979

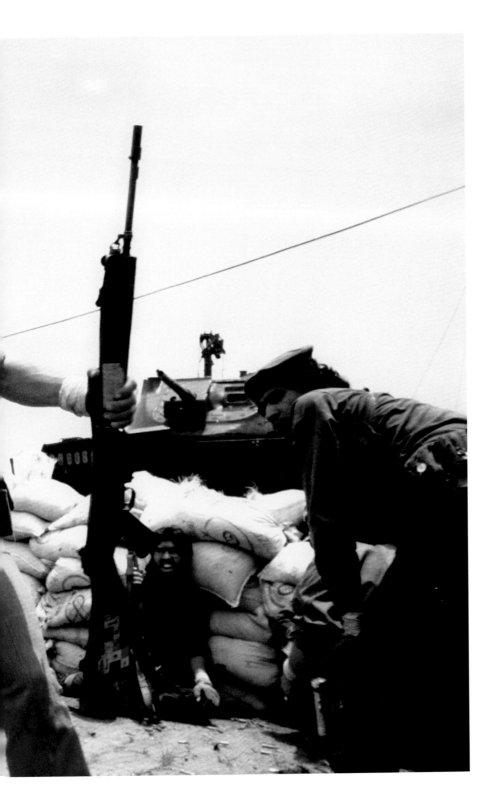

the continuous ambivalence as to who are you, and what are you in relationship to a violent political process. Are you simply a journalist? Can you be a sympathizer and a journalist? Are you a recorder, witness or an image-maker? I keep on remembering when I was asked in the mountains, 'Would you die for my country?' and I had said, 'No.' I reflect on the ambivalence as to whether I'm a messenger or a participant.

The Nicaraguans value the pictures as a memory. They have moved on and so are able to distance themselves from them. They print them on matchboxes, like the photograph of the young militant throwing a Molotov cocktail [pp. 92–93]. For me, there is the inevitable sadness of seeing photographs of people with guns, which have already lost the sense of who is inside them. I was left with these pictures and I felt I had completely failed, as they seemed so partial compared to what had been the whole experience.

When the war was going on, somehow you did not think that this was a war specific only to Nicaraguans. Its nationalism was temporarily suspended, as it were. After the victory, I felt separated. I was again an American, and the doors were beginning to close. The price of collecting information or news is at the cost of living like a human being. On the other hand, the price of becoming involved is that you may not be seen as a reliable witness. Sometimes I think that a photograph is instead of a relationship, and yet a photograph *is* a relationship.

So, as I said at the beginning of my letter, we may as well start at the end, when everybody was coming together with shared hopes and a past on which they hoped they would be able to base a future. It was the ending of a period of struggle, which had left 50,000 dead, cities totally devastated and an economy in ruins. There was no time to celebrate, there was no fiesta.

I had photographs, they have a revolution.

Right: Masaya, Nicaragua, July 1979

What was important – to me – was:

That the longest living dictatorship was defeated – by the people.

That the history of Nicaragua was spliced with that of the US, and that I hadn't ever been told that.

That that victory was earned – it had historical precedence and continuity.

That I think making a revolution is more important than making a story about a revolution.

But that's not to say that I don't think there's a function for the photographer in the making of a revolution. There's the whole question of the camera versus the gun; and at different stages what one does – what one chooses – what one says with a camera.

Something else about photographs – that, both for the people there and myself, they are still like souvenirs or landmarks…

So it's not so much what photographs are – but where they lead you.

That I was moved – that it was powerful to believe that something could change.

That I felt vital – and that I had a function. I felt the power of the media – when it's focused on and behind something. That period also clarified for me that no matter what is published, I cannot control it unless I create my own context for the work. My book had to live between and link distinct cultures.

I'm not sure that it's changed me but it's certainly clarified the relationships that exist in the world – I mean the powers that be – or the powers that exist and for whom. So it affirms for me who I align myself with – which is the people – which in English sounds terrible, but in Spanish doesn't. *El pueblo*. Perhaps because the masses have been identified for me there more than here.

– El Pueblo.

Right: Nicaragua, July 1979

# EL SALVADOR

In Nicaragua I mostly travelled alone in a car. In El Salvador I always teamed up with another local photographer, a writer, or somebody from TV. It was far too scary to be on the road alone. You could be eliminated without anyone knowing why or by whom. I had to stay in the central hotel for safety. There were protective alliances as well as competitive energy between the primetime media. There was the tension of trying to grab the scoop. If you left and planned not to come back that night, you made sure you told somebody. If I intended to cross the country to stay in a local hotel in a small town, I would tell someone not to worry. Then there were those people you wouldn't tell because you didn't know who they were really working for. You chose the people to confide in very carefully.

I would get up at five in the morning and mobilize. We would just choose a road and drive and see what we could find. One day in the early light the National Guard stopped a bus and were interrogating the passengers by the roadside. Not daring to point my camera directly at the scene, I photographed their shadows. There were certain places we went to every day which were dumping grounds for bodies. For example, El Playon was a famous lava field where you would just follow the smell or the vultures. I felt a strong need to be a witness. There had to be evidence; it felt urgent to document what was happening. At that point the magazines were very important partners in providing the immediacy of exposure.

It was often very difficult to get out of downtown San Salvador. You could drive up to certain regions and there would be heavy checkpoints and you'd be stopped from going down some main roads. If you were on a bus, and going from one town to another, you could be taken off and questioned. Significant areas of the country were completely controlled by the guerrillas so the military would have both offensive and defensive lines. You didn't always know where you were in relation to the two. The guerrillas

*Mano Blanca*, signature of the death squads, left on the door of a slain peasant organizer. Arcatao, El Salvador, 1980

Field training for Atlacatl Battalion by US advisors. El Salvador, 1983
Pages 102–3: Anonymous execution on the road to Usulután, El Salvador, 1981

would come down into a small town and attack the military post and take the town, not to keep it but just to demonstrate their strength. You could come across a situation like that without knowing. You had no cell phone, only the car radio, but who was reporting on the radio?

On December 3, 1980, we heard that four American churchwomen had been kidnapped close to the airport. The next day, we found their violated bodies. They had been targeted as they lived and worked with the poor. The crime resonated for decades. It took 17 years for the National Guardsmen who were convicted to acknowledge that they acted only after receiving 'orders from above', and it's only now, 35 years later, that the two presiding generals have been called to account and forced to flee their sanctuary in the US.

A month later I was driving some twenty miles north of San Salvador with the photographer John Hoagland and Ian Mates, a TV cameraman, when a landmine was detonated. John and I took shrapnel and I was lucky it just missed my eye. Another piece passed me and lodged in Ian's neck as he was driving. He died that night. We were naïve. We had no protection and just 'TV' stuck to the windshield with masking tape. The hardest thing at the time was becoming the centre of the story. We had been driving along a back road towards a town that had been taken and occupied by guerrillas. Now we were helicoptered out and arrived in Miami within forty-eight hours. You get used to crossfire. You know if it's incoming or outgoing, but mines are much darker and more terrifying. The deeper residue of the incident was that I didn't go back for months. There was a psychological aftermath and the accompanying paranoia.

Nearly a year later the guerrillas reported a massacre in the village of El Mozote, which the US State Department at first denied. Early in January 1982 I entered El

Salvador from Tegucigalpa in Honduras with Ray Bonner of *The New York Times*. We crossed the border and walked for several days through the northeastern province of Morazán, which was under rebel control. I saw exactly how the rebels' supply chain worked to receive food and water, weapons and ammunition. When we reached Mozote we found the reports of the massacre to be true. It had taken place on December 11, less than a month before. Homes had been burned down and bodies incinerated within them. The tiles of the roofs had collapsed around the corpses. Some of the bodies were decayed, some burned and others eaten by dogs. The only witness, Rufina Amaya, told us exactly what had happened in detail. The fact that the military were members of the Atlacatl Batallion, an elite unit trained in counterinsurgency and rapid deployment by the US Special Forces made the event even more shocking. Alma Guillermoprieto, writing for *The Washington Post*, arrived in Mozote shortly after us and the story became headline news in both *The New York Times* and the *Post*. It took a further ten years for Rufina Amaya's account to be proven by the bones that were exhumed. The big lesson for me was that I saw and photographed what seemed like evidence, but there was no way for me to confirm or prove the number of dead. Nearly a thousand villagers had been killed but we mostly came across burned fragments. Possession of the evidence can be endangering. We came out the way we came in. There had been a certainty about going to Mozote. We didn't focus on the risk. We felt we had to do it. We had to know what had happened.

I did not go back to El Salvador for an even longer period than before. I was frightened that publications might have revealed my name. Having just read about the disappeared and the Mothers of the Plaza de Mayo, I went instead to Argentina, where I could at least document the cemeteries. I felt compelled to focus on human rights abuses throughout Latin America.

By the mid-eighties there was a whole culture of terror. At that time I was still moving in and out of Nicaragua, and had gone back to working in El Salvador. In Nicaragua there had been a tremendous spirit of invention – such as with the literacy campaign that mobilized students to go to the countryside to educate *campesinos* – but, soon after, the US-backed Contras were fighting the Sandinista government by blowing up bridges and mining the harbours, crippling their country instead of transforming it, and in so doing undermined the population's confidence in the possibility of a different future. In El Salvador, meanwhile, there was the horror. What had been unleashed could not be turned around. My photographs seemed inadequate, and that inadequacy just grew. The frontline was a location of continual emotional turmoil for the population and for me.

# THE BORDER

The turmoil throughout the Central American isthmus at the end of the eighties left people desperate. There was the Contra war undermining the revolution in Nicaragua, an ongoing civil war in El Salvador, and militarization and horrific massacres of the Indian population in Guatemala. People tried to escape by illegally crossing the Mexican border into the US or by seeking political exile in Miami. I understood the impossibility of staying in the region. In 1989 when I went down to work with the US Border Patrol south of San Diego there was no resolution in place for any of those conflicts, or even hope that there could be one. The US border was extensive but not yet militarized. There was a growing debate and some determination to erect a steel wall and trench to protect America. I had seen a wire fence collapsing in California, but in the subsequent decades there has been still greater entrenchment, dividing Mexico and the rest of Central America from North America. It was not the physical barrier of the fence that interested me, but the idea of people crossing into a new world carrying their memory as well as the little else they had. I was especially drawn to the abandoned sites where people had been captured or had managed to escape and move on.

I started by using a 35mm camera and then changed to a Widelux, which has a lens that sweeps 180 degrees. It demands your eye anticipate and perform a kind of choreography with your body. I felt like it linked me to people, as I, in effect, followed their movement. The transitional sleeping and dreaming spaces intrigued me most. These places represented absence and the possibility for a transformation and an imagined future.

I exhibited the work under the title *Crossings*, weaving images from three narratives, in which the border series was at the centre, interrupted to create a memory landscape with colour from Nicaragua and black and white from El Salvador.

6:00 pm. US/Mexican border, Tijuana, Mexico, 1989

6:00 am. Search, Encinitas, California, 1989

11:00 am. 'Drop site' near Interstate 5, Oceanside, California, 1989

7:00 am. Flight from US Border Patrol, Encinitas, California, 1989

3:00 pm. Arrest alongside Interstate 5, Oceanside, California, 1989

# 3
## HISTORY

# RETURN TO NICARAGUA

The sense of the inadequacy of photographs in the face of the political force that challenged the revolution led me back to Nicaragua a decade later to find out what the people in the pictures felt about the photographs and what had happened in the ten years that had passed. I wanted to know in retrospect what their struggle meant and what the consequences had been. I had traced the life of many of the images I had made, but what did the pictures mean to their subjects? What did the 'Molotov Man' feel about being transformed into an historical icon? Another photograph placed several people in the same frame, but their lives had gone in different directions. Where were they now? I began by heading back, with the book, to the places I had made the photographs, and on each page noted what people knew about their neighbours' whereabouts.

The 'Molotov Man' was living up north. He'd had various jobs, from cutting lumber to working in an office, but in his mind he was still a Sandinista. I think he is proud to be the symbol of the revolution. I had wanted to find out if he felt trapped having to be that symbol. Was it possible for him to feel that the revolution had in some ways failed? For many people it has not turned out to be what they had dreamed of. For the people who were in the photographs, and for those to whom the photographs spoke of possibility, this was most difficult, as we share a world now stripped of hope.

On the 25th anniversary of the triumph over Somoza, I returned again, but this time with large murals of the same photographs to place them back in the landscape where they were made. I collaborated with the Institute of History at the local university. I wanted to further interrogate what photographs do and how they provoke collective memory; I especially wanted to know how they spoke to the next generation who had only heard about their history and not participated in it. The witness has always to protect memory from erasure. The murals provoke, and they perform that provocation publicly. Time and the world's attention move on.

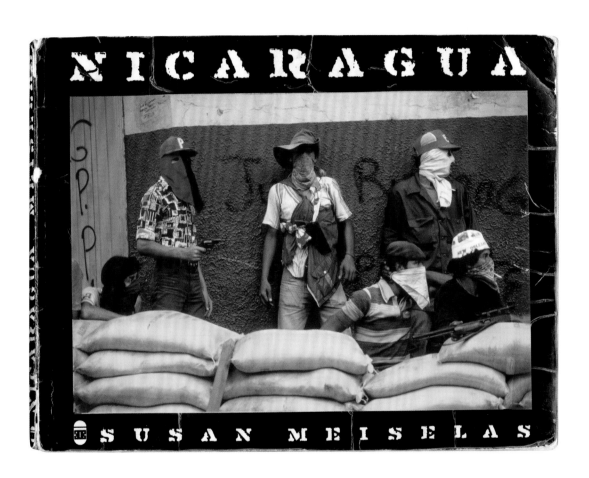

Cover of *Nicaragua: June 1978–July 1979*, published by Pantheon, 1981; Aperture, 2008, 2016

134

Left & above: Annotated *Nicaragua: June 1978–July 1979*, with field notes from the search for original subjects in photographs for the film *Pictures from a Revolution* (co-directed by Susan Meiselas, Richard P. Rogers and Alfred Guzzetti), July 1991
Pages 136–37: Mural featuring Nicaraguan folk legends including the 'Molotov Man'. Masaya, Nicaragua, 1986
Pages 138–39: Wall stencil mobilizing popular militia against the Contras, based on 'Molotov Man'. Matagalpa, Nicaragua, 1984

The image of youths practising throwing
contact bombs in forest surrounding Monimbo,
June 1978, from the series *Reframing History*,
exhibited in Monimbo, Nicaragua, July 2004

*Muchacho* withdrawing from commercial district after three days of bombing, Masaya, September 1978, from the series *Reframing History*, Masaya, Nicaragua, July 2004

MASAYA, 1978

Cuesta del Plomo, site of assassinations carried out
by the National Guard, Managua, June 1978,
from the series *Reframing History*, Managua,
Nicaragua, July 2004

# KURDISTAN

In 1991 I went to Kurdistan knowing very little about the region. I had spent over a decade in Latin America. This was a leap to what I thought would be different, and then it turned out that I began just where I left off. I didn't go to Kurdistan knowing how long I might stay or what project might evolve. I was drawn to it magnetically. But, looking back now, I could never have done what I did, beginning with crossing a border illegally, had I not done something like that before. I already had a sense of who to trust and how to travel. There was the same urgency and necessity to witness. Again, the calling had to do with the fact that something horrific had happened, and again the concept of the project evolved in the field.

There had been a Kurdish insurrection in Northern Iraq, provoked to some degree by President George H. W. Bush, though the US then offered no support. The Kurds were fleeing from Northern Iraq into Turkey, and a good many into Iran. Most of the coverage was focused on conditions in Turkey, where it was easier for a reporter to get a visa. In March 1991 I had read reports by Middle East Watch (which later became part of Human Rights Watch) that gave accounts of refugee testimonies about the destruction of four thousand villages, but there was no visual evidence. Middle East Watch told me about Bakhtiar Amin, a Kurd who was heading for Paris on an Air France flight out of JFK. I was already booked on a flight out of Newark but managed to switch. I boarded the Air France flight and found Bakhtiar and we talked all night.

Magnum Paris managed to come up with a letter saying that I was in effect a citizen of the world working from their office, and this I presented at the Iranian consulate. As I was standing in line I wondered why all the media people were there. It turned out that Madame Mitterrand was going to Iran. All the press seats on her flight were taken, so I got a five-day visa and took a flight to Tehran. I didn't even think to bring a *chador*, but a British Airways stewardess gave me her long blue

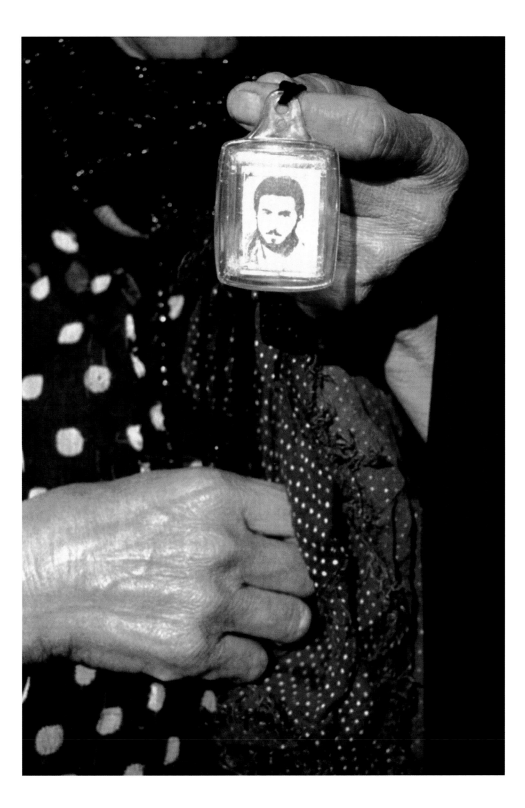

smock and told me to stay at Tehran airport until I could pick up a local flight to the border. Immediately upon arrival in Haji Omran, the Iranian police took me aside and interrogated me. Even though I had a visa, my presence and the fact that I was an American were suspicious. I asked them, 'Don't you know Madame Mitterrand is coming?' These situations are stressful, as you don't know what they're thinking, and you don't have a common language so there's little means of communication and no one else to turn to. By the time Madame Mitterrand's plane arrived many hours later, there was such a circus that they forgot about me and I just joined her entourage.

The main purpose of Madame Mitterrand's visit was to get food and clothing to the Kurdish refugees camped out on the Iranian border with Iraq. The Iranians were annoyed that the Turks were getting so much attention. I had no idea what she was going to do with the refugees and just followed her as she began to walk across a minefield. The Iranian police were going crazy but she was determined to get to the actual border. She had made a date with Masoud Barzani, the head of the Kurdish KDP. As we were proceeding, these magnificently dressed Peshmerga – literally 'those who face death', members of the Kurdish militia – came up a hill from Kurdistan, accompanied by dazzling women in long sequinned robes. They all sat down in the middle of the minefield and had a tea party. I tried to photograph Madame Mitterrand but the midday sun shadowed her face and made it nearly impossible. Then, as I looked around, astonishingly I saw that her translator turned out to be none other than Bakhtiar, the Kurd I'd met on the flight to Paris.

After the meeting ended, I took Bakhtiar to one side and asked if he could arrange for me to go back with the Peshmerga into Kurdistan. He quickly spoke with someone and shortly after that I went back with them across the border, which was just after Saddam's troops had retreated to Baghdad. I was travelling through what felt like a

Right: Entry to former women's prison of Saddam Hussein, Sulaymaniyah, Northern Iraq, 2007

liberated zone. It was not an active front. In the following few days I documented the genocidal campaign known as the Anfal. The Kurds took me to every village they could and I noted the remains of each distinct place, despite their appearing the same as mere piles of rubble. We eventually reached Qala Diza, a town that had once had a population of over 60,000 people, but which had been systematically destroyed. After that, they took me back and I walked across the border, flew to Tehran and on to Paris. It was my first trip to Kurdistan. If I hadn't had the experience of being around a lot of guns in Latin America, I would never have gotten into a car with armed Peshmerga. I was compelled by the search for evidence.

Returning several months later, I discovered that the Peshmerga had entered the military bases and seized eighteen tons of Iraqi intelligence files. Embedded in these documents were photographs, many of them ID pictures that had been in the pockets of those the military had executed. The ID photographs were resonant. Who were these people? Why were they seen as threatening to Saddam? The ID images represented the loss felt by the mothers of the dead, much as they did for the mothers of the missing I had met in Argentina. But here they also represented a presence behind the desire for a defined homeland. Could you tell their history through which images survived?

The search and uncovering of images led me to think of myself in a long line of image-makers who had travelled to and from Kurdistan. Aside from local studio photographers, there were many missionaries, colonial administrators and anthropologists. Each had a particular relationship to the Kurds, and photographs marked and revealed their distinct missions. In the 1890s, Ernest Chantre made forensic studies of skulls, which would now be considered racial profiling of the Kurds. In 1919 Major E. W. Noel travelled across Turkey with the photographer Percival Richards, who left his handwritten comments on the back of his photographs. Noel wrote a defining text about the relations between the Turks and the Kurds. Those tensions are still evident in the two cultures. Was co-existence an impossibility? Noel was travelling just after the Sykes-Picot Agreement of 1916, which established the boundaries of what became the modern state of Turkey. At the same time Major Ely Banister Soane brought his 19-year-old wife Lynette, who had a camera, and she photographed Adela Khanum, one of the great women leaders of Kurdish history. It became important to gather images of these personal meetings, alongside dramatic events like the hanging of Qazi Muhammad in 1947. Though people had heard of his death, they had never seen the photograph.

I became preoccupied by the idea that 'pictures are made and taken away', so a culture might not get to see itself. There is also the issue of what happens after an image is made. I began to backtrack to Western archives and family collections to discover where a photograph of a Kurd might be – out in the world, lost, buried in a depository. Then I felt an additional sense of responsibility to repatriate what I had found. The burial released the metaphor for uncovering Kurdistan, which lives in the act of digging. The digging unleashed an obsessive gene that drove me to search for what had gone missing, and what remained unknown. The trawling through the archives was parallel with the witnessing and the actual exhumation of graves.

Pages 152–53: Families return to the ruins of their homes after the Iraqi army forced them to leave in 1989. Qala Diza, Northern Iraq, April 1991
Pages 154–55: Destroyed village along the Hamilton Road, Northern Iraq, 1991
Pages 156–57: Village cemetery, Jeznikam-Beharke, Northern Iraq, 1991
Pages 158–59: Concrete blocks mark the mass grave in Koreme, Northern Iraq, 1992
Pages 160–61: Clothing, unearthed in the search for identification of those buried anonymously, marks graves, Arbil cemetery, Northern Iraq, December 1991
Pages 162–63: Shards of canisters left after a chemical attack by Saddam Hussein during the Anfal campaign of May 1988. Goptapa, Northern Iraq, 1992
Pages 164–65: Refugees living in a deserted former military base, Qasir and Macos, Northern Iraq, 1991
Pages 166–67: Refugees in Said Sadiq, Northern Iraq, June 1992
Pages 168–69: Gravestone of Peshmerga martyr, Saiwan Hill cemetery, Arbil, Northern Iraq, December 1991
Pages 170–71: Family members wear photographs of Peshmerga martyrs, Saiwan Hill cemetery, Arbil, Northern Iraq, December 1991

As you dig, you question. Who am I to select? Who am I to bring back the past? I joined, and also created, an elaborate network of scholars and researchers. The gathering of material was a circular, encompassing process rather than simply a selection of what I valued aesthetically. The method demanded a compression of history, which had been shaped by the geographical borders – namely the decisive and seemingly arbitrary division by the Sykes-Picot Agreement, still contested today. This conflict seems as endless as the Kurdish longing for nationhood. I found myself trying to make sense of history in the face of the infinite. I was looking at the image of the person whose life had been intercepted by the photographer, but I was also looking at how the photographer must have been marked or impacted by those encounters.

The book that emerged is non-linear because you can open it at any spread and discover a collage of elements that are independent from the overriding chronology. I saw it as a mosaic of fragments, not as a conventional or definitive history. There was no thematic treatment: the book reveals the fabric of women's lives, for example, but there is no chapter specifically on women. The aesthetic choices were counterbalanced by contextualizing primary materials. I wanted to provoke the reader to think about the larger historical framework with small contributions both authored and anonymous. I also wanted the reader to feel time at work – literally, in the shift of tones, from warm sepia to cooler black and white and then colour, from autochromes to Kodachrome.

The photographs in the book on Nicaragua were all made by me; in Kurdistan I was a small part in a long timeline. In Nicaragua I was presenting a history I had lived and the photographs stood for what I had seen, as opposed to the hundred years of history in Kurdistan of which I have experienced only a tiny part; in the latter I was looking for the photographs by others who had witnessed history. In the Nicaragua book I was aware that I had only included seventy-one photographs and there was only

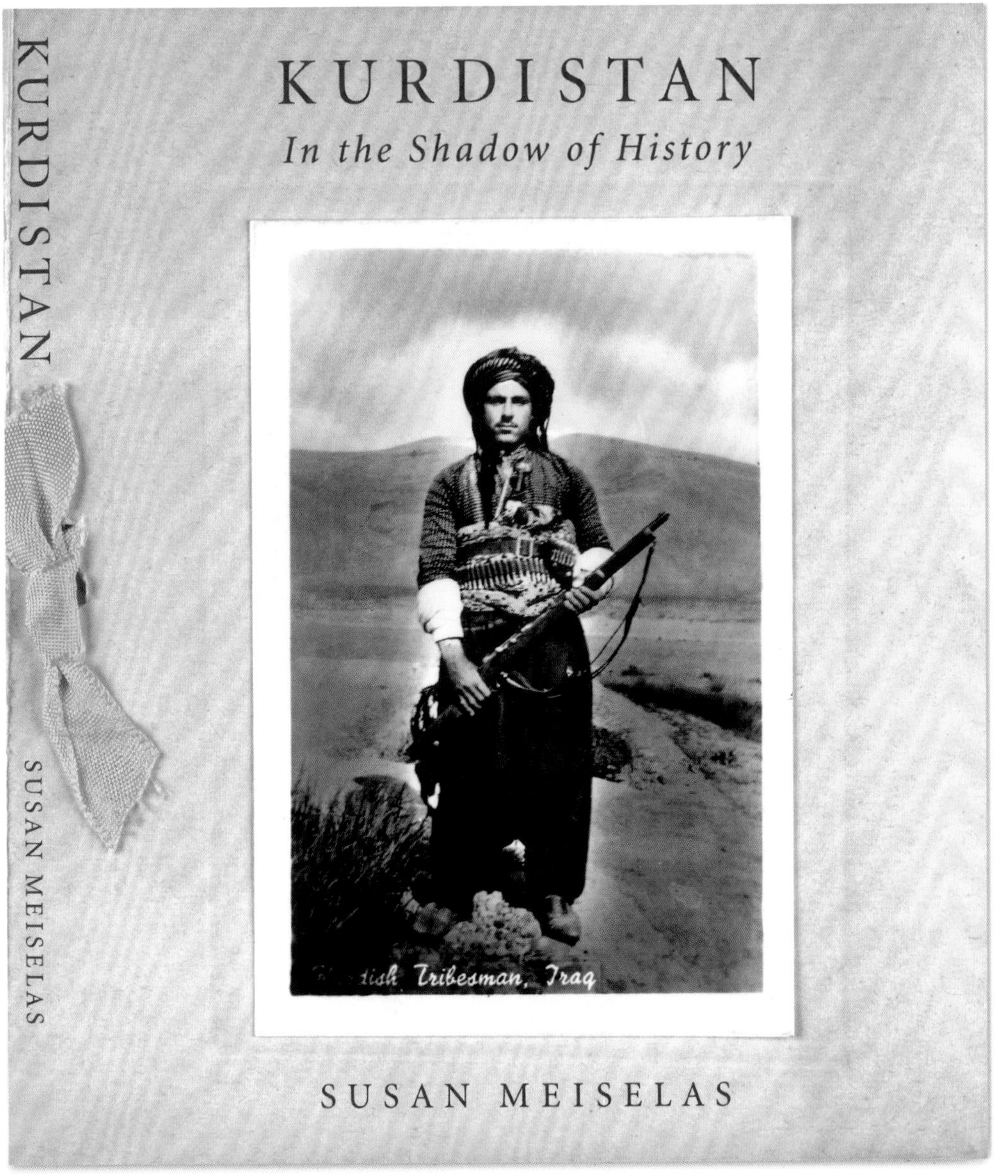
KURDISTAN
In the Shadow of History
KURDISTAN
SUSAN MEISELAS
Tribesman, Iraq
SUSAN MEISELAS

*Kurdistan: In the Shadow of History*, published by Random House, 1997; University of Chicago Press, 2008
Pages 174–77: Scrapbooks with preparatory research for *Kurdistan: In the Shadow of History*, 1995
Pages 178–81: Page spreads from *Kurdistan: In the Shadow of History*, Random House, 1997

Salut de l'Orient

1610 TYPES DE SYRIE. — Guerriers Kurdes. LL.

Missions des Lazaristes

Famille Kurde

PERSE — Un Kurde, chef de tribu

Femmes Kurdes de Djoulfa

KURDISTAN.
43. Typical Kurd.

Ow-Po-
Ow-Po-1245-25
Bjw-Pn-1245-105

- Interview with Mimi Doretti

- Letter from Joost Hiltermann

excerpt from The New

# The New York Times Magazine

JANUARY 3, 1993 / SECTION 6

## IRAQ
A CASE OF GENOCIDE
## ACCUSED
BY JUDITH MILLER

Martyrs of the Koreme massacre, from KDP archive

excerpts from Human Rights Watch Reports

**P. D. K**

الحزب الديمقراطي الكردستاني

نەمری بۆشە هيدێت گوندێ كوريێئ و
سەركاروانێ شەهيدا ئارزانی نەمر.

# THE ANFAL CAMPAIGN IN IRAQI KURDISTAN

more of
Amnesty
interview
coming

looking for original
drawings still
+ notes from field

The Destruction of Koreme

**Middle East Watch**
A DIVISION OF HUMAN RIGHTS WATCH
**Physicians for Human Rights**

Btw-D- 1009772

Dearest,

The political officers and myself are at present living in the Khanum's house, and having a pretty good time. The Lady herself is about sixty-five years of age. But she dyes her hair and paints and powders her face, and on the whole, tries to play the giddy young thing. However she must be very strong willed, because her tribe (before the coming of the British) were nothing but highway robbers, and yet she had 'em in the palm of her hand to do just what she liked with—some woman! . . .

Within a radius of say, a hundred miles each way, the political and myself are absolutely the only two Englishmen to be found. The population is Kurdish, and they have no written language, so we have to rely on what we can pick up. . . . We live just absolutely the same as the Kurds (they live extraordinarily well by the way) and rather like it. . . .

The job is no sinecure, as the population is almost wholly nomad (like me) and it is no easy thing to keep them in order and make them pay their taxes and things. We have a force of gendarmerie recruited from amongst the tribes to keep law and order, and very stout fellows the gendarmes are (set a thief to catch a thief is the British Policy).

Letter from Percival Richards
to his wife, December 20, 1919
Courtesy Richard Hesketh

Dear respected and faithful friend,

You left and broke both our circle and our heart. Only God knows how much sorrow has come into my heart because of the departure of you dear; especially so, because I did not know how far you've gotten. When your letter arrived from Bombay, how happy I became. May you be happy because you made our day. You had kindly asked about me. Fortunately, there is no grief except for the sorrow of you being away. I hope that soon in utmost health and joy you will return to your country, see your friends and be gratified. God willing, hasten your return so that I may once more be happy seeing you. Let me know how you are. Waiting to hear from you, dear.

Wife of Othman Pasha

Seal given by the British reads
"Khan Bahadur Adela"
Letter from Adela Khanum to Lynette
Soane, Major E. B. Soane's wife, 1920,
translated by Amir Hassanpour
Courtesy Sheri Laizer

Adela Khanum (Lynette Soane is seated to her left) surrounded by her family, 1920

Percival Richards/
Courtesy Richard Hesketh

ELY (in centre) AND SOME OF HIS STAFF. KURDISTAN 1920

CAPTAIN LEES GUARD ON A MOUNTAIN SIDE

THOSE WITH CROSSES SINCE

DEAD

ELY (DIED AT SEA) 1923

CAPT FITZGIBBON MURDERED

IN KURDISTAN 1921

CAPT BOND MURDERED

1922

CAPT MAKANT MURDERED 1922

CAPT WRIGHT

KILLED NORTH AFRICA

1925.

SELF. PRINCESS ADELA. ELY, CAPT LEES & HAMAD BEG

TAKEN AT HALABJA KURDISTAN SEPT 1924

Handwritten captions and photographs by Lynette Soane/Courtesy Sheri Laizer

Major Soane came as an Oriental and stayed in the area. He had contacts with a lot of the tribal heads in the area, such as the Jaf and the Pishdar. At that time, it was not Iraq but Mesopotamia. There were three vilayets—Basra, Baghdad, and Mosul, the Kurdish vilayet. Shaikh Mahmud rose up for the rights of the Kurds, but international policy did not allow for this at the time, and the British brought Major Soane back. Major Soane was a political advisor to Shaikh Mahmud, but secretly he was contacting the heads of the tribes in Kurdistan and organizing them against him.

The day Major Soane came back, Shaikh Mahmud went to receive him. From the moment they met, Shaikh Mahmud realized, from the way Soane shook his hand, that he was coming to demolish Shaikh Mahmud's government.

The division of Kurdistan didn't start then. It started when Sykes and Picot sat at the table and divided the country in 1916. The British planned through the Orientalists how to create problems if anything endangered the division they had decided on.

Interview with Shaikh Salar Hafid, Shaikh Mahmud's grandson, living in Iraq, May 1993

TEATRO ALLA SCALA - LEILA BEDIRKHAN
*Ricyton di Sabaj nel ballo "Belkis"*
FOT. M. CAMUZZI
DELLA S.A. CRIMELLA

*Princess Leila performing at La Scala Theater*

M. Camuzzi/Kurdish Institute of Paris

## Leila Bedirkhan
### Kurdish Dancer

*I'm not Persian . . . I'm a Kurd.
My grandfather was the crown
prince of Kurdistan, which is on
the frontier between Persia,
Turkey and Syria.*

*But since the Turkish conquest,
the independent princes in our
family have become spread over
a wide area. I was born in Turkey,
in Constantinople. When I was
very young, I left for Egypt with
my mother and spent my
childhood there. I only came to
Europe after the war, to study in
Switzerland.*

*I've always loved dancing.
In Egypt, when I was a child, I
learned it through instinct, by
watching the common women
dancing.*

*I don't learn my dances.
I dance instinctively using very
stylized popular themes. I also
invent dances. . . . As you can see,
they have no specific origin. . . .
I don't use my legs much when
I'm dancing; I mainly use my
arms and my body.*

Helene Bory, "The Kurdish Princess
Leila Bedirkhan Talks to Us About Her
Dances and Women of the Orient,"
Paris Midi, December 16, 1932

*Dancing was just a pastime for
me when I was a child, something
I enjoyed doing—in the same way
others learn to play the piano or
to do embroidery (which I also
learned to do, by the way). When,
after the tragic death of my father,
the Emir, I fled from my revolt-
stricken country, dancing became
my very reason for living, my life's
aim. I traveled through Austria,
Germany, and Switzerland;
after some early performances in
most of the large cities in these
countries, I settled in Paris where,
after two recitals, I decided
to spend a year researching the
religious rites of ancient
Persia, Egyptian Mazdeism
[Zoroastrism], Indian, and
Oriental sacred dances.*

Comedia, December 9, 1930

Right: "Kurdistan Princess
Reveals Harem Dances!"

Unknown/UPI/Corbis-Bettmann, New York

WATCH YOUR CREDIT.......
FL 12376'               "P & A PHOTOS"
(PHOTO SHOWS PRINCESS LEILA)

KURDISTAN PRINCESS REVEALS HAREM DANCES!

     PRINCESS LEILA, DAUGHTER OF THE LAST
EMIR OF KURDISTAN, WHO WAS INITIATED INTO THE
~~SEXRED~~ SACRED DANCES OF THE HAREM, IS RE-
VEALING THEIR MYSTERIES AND IS NOW DANCING
PUBLICLY IN A PARIS THEATRE. SHE RECENTLY
PAID A VISIT TO LONDON. PHOTO SHOWS PRINCESS
LEILA WEARING ONE OF THE DRESSES SPECIALLY
MADE FOR HER BY PAUL POIRET, THE DESIGNER.
          (B NY 12-31-26)

so much each could portray; the Kurdistan book has 400 pages, in which only a dozen photographs are by me.

For me the selection of photographs from the Nicaragua book have now become a reference set fixed in time. In the case of Kurdistan my intention was to go beyond the boundaries of the book to the internet, which, when we started in 1998, was on the cusp of endless possibilities. There was the opportunity to inspire the sharing of contributions in order to continue gathering a collective memory. I imagined a site where anyone was invited to send in pictures and stories from any part of Kurdistan. Since then, that ongoing participation has grown, and instead of a digital exchange I've created a painted wall map of the region and Europe without defining Kurdish borders. There are now small story books, hanging on hooks, from the Kurdish diaspora and others. I hope some day there will be a small square room where the whole world is seen inside out and the stories of the Kurds will be suspended from the map that encloses you.

When the Kurdistan book was finished in 1997, no one imagined what would happen within the next ten years – that Saddam would be dead, that there would be a Kurdish president and that the Kurds would have an autonomous region in Iraq, despite the bitter conflict still raging. Who knew that Syria would unravel with nearly a decade of devastating destruction?

Because of the wars, I couldn't take the book back to Kurdistan, which would have been a gesture of return. The second edition, printed in 2008, updated the history. It also provided the opportunity to add a section in Sorani, the Central Kurdish language, and Turkish. But the books were banned in Turkey so we couldn't simply drive trucks with boxes over the border to Kurdistan. The Italian printers, Mondadori, still had the plates from the original printers' film, but their digital press in Italy could no longer use them, so the book had to be reprinted in Spain. Copies were shipped by boat to Dubai and then sent as airfreight straight to Kurdistan. I arrived to help distribute them to libraries, universities, families and all who had contributed.

A photograph is always a record of a relationship. People had contributed photographs they had made or found and given them to a stranger in the interests of a history that was very precious to them. The cycle of return of what had been generously shared felt complete.

Pages 184–85: Page spread from *Kurdistan: In the Shadow of History*, showing Qala Diza, 1991, in comparison to Qala Diza, 2007, Northern Iraq, November 2007
Pages 186–87: Amusement park for domestic tourism, Rowanduz, Northern Iraq, November 2007
Pages 188–89: Pool of oil, 40 metres (130 ft) deep, Tawke, Northern Iraq, November 2007

U.S.A. $100.00
Canada $140.00

184

Charred copy of *Kurdistan: In the Shadow of History*, retrieved from the ruins of a Kurdish community centre in London that had been torched by arsonists, August 1998

# KURDISTAN
## In the Shadow of History

tish Tribesman, Iraq

## SUSAN MEISELAS

# 4
## THE INTERIOR

# THE DANI

In the early sixties the anthropologist Robert Gardner made a very important film, *Dead Birds*, about the indigenous people of the Baliem Valley in the highlands of Indonesia. Gardner was able to stay for six months in the valley to film. He was documenting the lives of what were essentially Stone Age people, and he also produced a book, *Gardens of War*. He heard that 'eco-tourists' had been visiting the area and they brought copies of the book to the Dani, but they never brought the film. Gardner decided to go back for the first time in late 1988, and invited Dick Rogers and me to accompany him.

Gardner returned to the community that had welcomed him decades before. Pua, a boy who had been seven years old, was now in his thirties. The Dani had never seen the film or the stills. There was an almost confessional moment when Gardner put the photographs in their hands. Of course one moves on. Going back opens up a new set of questions about what has happened in the meantime. The Indonesians had exercised their power and the culture of the Dani had been eroded. They were forbidden to remain naked. The young men were being assimilated and acquiring a new identity.

We went back again seven years later, and then the change really struck me. I wanted to go beyond my own pictures and track the gradual impact of encounters with the outside world, but in the highlands there was nothing to find. There were no family albums, no trace of a history. The search had to be conducted outside their culture by turning to sources in archives and books, and finding fragments to assemble. By 2000 I could also use the internet. Situated in New York, at a perfect point between the time zones, I could communicate with a network of academics and travellers both in Europe and in Asia. I found a lot of surprising documents, including a comic book, and a memoir of an American woman marrying a Dani chief. The Dani themselves were no longer resisting. They wanted to be modern and they were being progressively decimated in the process.

Dani lookout point, Baliem Valley, Irian Jaya, Indonesia, 1989
Pages 196 & 197: Members of the Dani tribe with Robert Gardner, American filmmaker, director of *Dead Birds*,
who returned to Irian Jaya 30 years after making his film about the tribe, Baliem Valley, Indonesia, 1989
Pages 198–99: Mummy displayed in the village of Akima, Baliem Valley, Indonesia, 1989
Pages 200–1: Cultural festival and war re-enactment in Pyramid, Indonesia, 1996

# COVA DA MOURA

A curator in Portugal was interested in looking at how her country had been seen over time by reviewing the digital archive of photographers in Magnum. This was not unrelated to my thoughts and approach in gathering the history of Kurdistan. Henri Cartier-Bresson, Martin Parr and Gilles Peress were among those whose work from earlier decades was to be included in a show. Three of us – Miguel Rio Branco, Josef Koudelka and myself – were given open commissions to make new pictures. Josef made a series of landscapes and Miguel had lived in Portugal and made a kind of collage, drawing on his childhood memory. I had no bearings or entry point of experience to draw on. The most astounding fact I discovered was that Portugal had only one per cent racial diversity. How would it feel to be part of that one per cent? My first few days were spent trying to uncover where one could find that one per cent.

Obviously the one per cent were for the most part of African descent, and there were some Latin Americans. They were mostly from the former colonies. So I had to follow the history. Who could resettle in Portugal? Spain had previously received many immigrants from Latin America, but Portugal was more isolated. Unlike Germany, France or even Spain, Portugal doesn't draw immigrants. I found a few markets in Lisbon where Africans were selling fruit. I also heard of settlements on the outskirts and of some organizations working on behalf of immigrants. One was called SOS Racism. I made an appointment, and walked into their office to find a single man at a desk piled with papers and clearly overwhelmed. As I waited for him to finish a phone call I saw a blue pamphlet on 'Tourism in Cova da Moura'. I had heard that the youth association of that neighbourhood, on the fringe of the city, was inviting people to visit. So I simply decided to go the next morning.

Cova was a compact maze of squatters on a hillside. They didn't have land rights. Most of the residents came from the former colonies of Cape Verde or Angola. The

Night watch, Cova da Moura, Portugal, 2004

district was known for drug dealing and had a bad reputation. Outsiders were warned not to venture in. I met with the people from the youth association and, in order to see my way around the maze, I was told to go at night, when I could be driven through the small streets to get a sense of the dense quarter. I then returned the next day with a young translator who spoke Spanish and Portuguese. We tried just walking around and were immediately challenged. 'Who are you?' or 'You don't belong here'. To say I was an American wouldn't help. Simply being white and curious could be perceived as spying or gathering information that might be of value to somebody else. I realized it was a very defined and separate world. I wondered what I'd be able to find if I stayed. I only had three weeks to work and I knew the size of the gallery that I was supposed to fill at the Museum of Modern Art in Lisbon.

At that time (2004) the first little cell phones were appearing with a minimal capacity to make low-resolution photographs. The kids, some of whom used them for drug deals, all had those phones. I was fascinated because my phone couldn't take pictures. I had come with an SX-70 and quickly realized that they had never seen a Polaroid picture and were intrigued by the magical process and its beautiful quality. As I met people in the neighbourhood, I made the point of giving them the pictures, and writing their name and the date when I signed them.

Six months later, when the exhibition was to be held in the white museum box, I knew that none of the kids would go. A museum just didn't mean anything to them. I felt I had to work on a parallel project with the teenagers to coincide with the museum show. First I went house to house throughout Cova to find the Polaroids I had given away to ask if we could reproduce them as murals. The idea was that they could choose where they wanted to hang them, either on the streets or outside their homes. We also went back to the various community settings, like the club where they played cards or where there was a fashion show, to include them in the murals. Then I brought back small point-and-shoot digital cameras to begin a collaboration making new photographs. We had a workshop to show the participants how to photograph. By the time of the festival of São João (or 'Kola San Jon'), they had hung their pictures with string and laundry clips around a tower in the centre of town. They signed them and celebrated what they'd made. I think by then they also could see themselves in the photographs I'd made. Many people of Lisbon came to Cova for the first time and were guided by the kids through what was previously an impenetrable world. The community, which was at best invisible or marginal, became part of a larger culture simply by seeing and sharing themselves.

Left & pages 208–13: Cova da Moura, Portugal, 2004

213

Décio          11.30.04

*Chalecha e Zaguinha*
*11.29.04*

Left: Décio, Cova da Moura, Portugal, 2004
Above: Chalecha and Zaguinha, Cova da Moura, Portugal, 2004

Left & pages 218–19: Mural projects
displayed in Cova da Moura,
Portugal, June 2005

Vânia e Vanessa

# ARCHIVES OF ABUSE

I began working with the San Francisco police to see how their daily rounds related to domestic violence. I was one of several artists commissioned to visualize the issue in some way, to give it a more public profile, in that there was so much denial about the subject at that time. I had come across some shocking statistics:

1.  Every year it is estimated that 2.1 million married, separated or divorced women in the US are beaten by their partners (Patrick Langan, Christopher Innes: Bureau of Justice Statistics Special Report, 'Preventing Domestic Violence Against Women', Washington, DC, US Department of Justice, August 1986, p. 3).

2.  The FBI reports that almost 1/3 of all female homicide victims in the US are killed by a husband or boyfriend (FBI Uniform Crime Reports, 1988).

3.  22–35% of women going to hospital emergency rooms are there because of domestic violence (JAMA [Journal of the American Medical Association], August 22/29, 1990, Vol. 264, No. 8, p. 943).

4.  Battering is the single-most major cause of violence/injury to women, even more major than the numbers injured in muggings, rapes or auto accidents combined (J. O'Reilly, 'Wife Beating: Silent Crime', *Time* magazine, September 5, 1983).

5.  91% of spouse abuse victims are women (P. Klaus, M. Rand: Bureau of Justice Statistics Special Report, 'Family Violence', Washington, DC, US Department of Justice, 1984, p. 4).

The idea behind the project was to create awareness about a new crisis line and reveal the scale of incidence. My instinct was to start with the evidence – sometimes found in hotel rooms, sometimes in homes. The evidence was on the walls, the clothing and the bodies. I worked alongside the police and waited with them. It was

Right: Untitled III, San Francisco, California, 1991

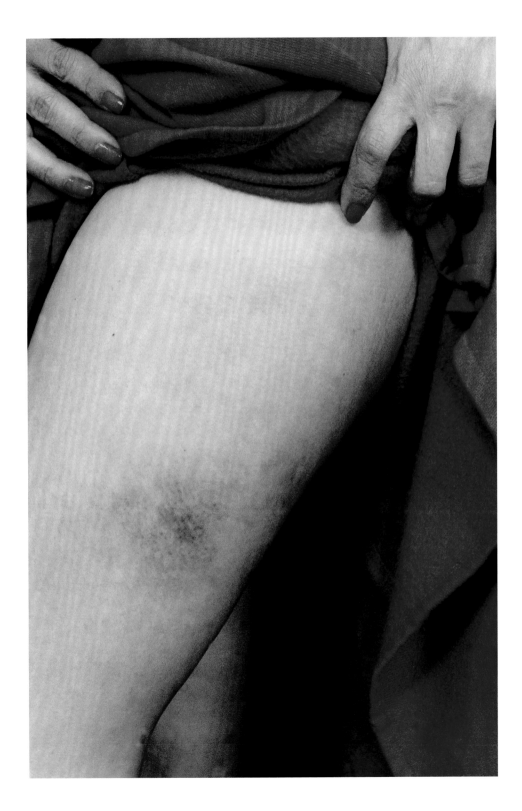

INCIDENT NO    ████████████    REPORTING OFFICER ████████    STAR ███    DATE(S) & TIME(S) OF OCCURRENCE   10-21-91, 1730 - 10-22-91, 0130

NARRATIVE: SUBSEQUENT TO CLEANING UP HER
RESIDENCE AFTER HER EX-HUSBAND VANDALIZED IT, ████
████████ FOUND THE FOLLOWING WRITTEN ON HER KITCHEN
FLOOR, "DON'T FUCK W/A CRAZY MAN I'LL TEACH YOU
██████████████████ YOU'LL BE DEAD BEFORE ANY OF THIS
MATTERS. I LOVED YOU, HOW MUCH. YOU SHOULD HAVE GONE OUT
W/ME BECAUSE I WANT TO DIE NOW + I'M GOING TO TAKE YOU
W/ME I WON'T LET YOU BE WITH ANOTHER MAN! I'M SORRY
BUT YOU HAVE TO GO TO HEAVEN W/ME."

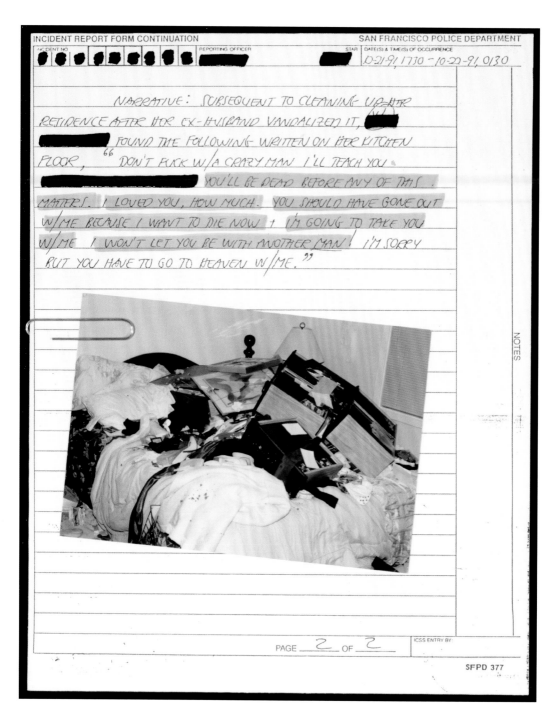

NOTES

PAGE ___2___ OF ___2___    ICSS ENTRY BY:

SFPD 377

a slow but progressive process. In folders on their desks the police kept handwritten reports from the site of a crime, together with testimonies of whoever had spoken to them – a neighbour, a parent. They wrote down the essence of what they were told, in a methodical way, like scribes. I was struck by the power of their reports which was derived from such compressed language. I began to wonder what they did with the reports, which led me to the District Attorney's office, where the evidence for the court trials was gathered. The city of San Francisco was taking a very radical position at that time by believing they should prosecute on behalf of the victims regardless of whether or not the victims were willing to participate. I told the DA's office that I wanted to reveal their work by taking the visual evidence they held in order to attach it to their written reports, which I then photographed as assembled documents or collages. Before presenting them, I checked with the victims to be sure they accepted to be part of such public display. Within a few months, a bus-shelter poster that combined an image and text was made and placed all over the city announcing the first women's crisis line.

Originally I wanted to do something more aggressive or provocative than use images on bus shelters, despite the tremendous visibility and the fact that at least the posters were functional – they provided information for a helpline; they confronted those who didn't know domestic violence was really happening. I actually wanted to put pictures of women in the dressing rooms of a department store in the main square of the city, where other women would be trying on clothes. As they rehoused their bodies in whatever costume they chose, they would have to think about the body of a woman who had been violated.

Left & page 225: Collage of police report with crime scene, San Francisco, California, 1992
Pages 226–27: Aftermath in hotel, San Francisco, California, 1991

I recognized the power of absence within these archives of abuse. I imagined the places where things had happened, and discovered the emptiness of the aftermath image. A scar or wound is evidence, but the place itself is only really known to the person on whom the violence was inflicted. It exists in memory. This resonated with previous work on civil conflict or the tearing apart of families – some members migrating, some living, some dead. How do people move on? How do they let go of what has happened to them? How does anyone go beyond the violence that has been perpetrated? How does anyone live within the landscapes of their memory?

| INCIDENT NO | REPORTING OFFICER | STAR | DATE(S) & TIME(S) OF OCCURRENCE |
|---|---|---|---|
| 🖤🖤🖤🖤🖤🖤🖤🖤 | ▬▬ | ▬ | 2.27.91 0030 / 2.27.91 0700 |

VICTIM CODES CONT ▬▬ ▬▬ 52

2 ▬▬

R# ▬▬

R#4 ▬▬

NARRA▬▬ TO

22▬▬

Wh▬▬ ME

TO v/▬▬ REAR DOOR

AND I ▬▬ FLOOR,

SHE W▬▬ ▬▬

BLOOD ON ▬▬ AND

I H81 AR▬▬

COULD NO▬▬

CAME RUN ▬▬ THY SAID HIS MOM WAS
LAYING ON THE FLOOR BLEEDING. ▬▬ SAID SHE CALLED
THE POLICE AND THEN RAN TO ▬▬ HOUSE.
▬▬ SAID HE WOKE UP THIS MORNING AND WAS
GETTING READY FOR SCHOOL WHEN HE WENT DOWNSTAIRS AND
FOUND HIS MOTHER PASSED OUT ON THE FLOOR AND BLEEDING FROM
THE HEAD. ▬▬ TOLD ME HE RAN TO ▬▬
HOUSE TO CALL THE POLICE BECAUSE THE PHONE LINES IN HIS HOUSE
WERE CUT. ▬▬ STATED THE PHONE WAS WORKING AND THE
LINES WERE FINE WHEN HE WENT TO BED LAST NIGHT. ▬▬
TOLD ME SHE CONVERSED WITH ▬▬ VIA PHONE LAST NIGHT
AT APPROXIMATELY 0001 HRS.    PAGE __2__ OF __4__

NOTES

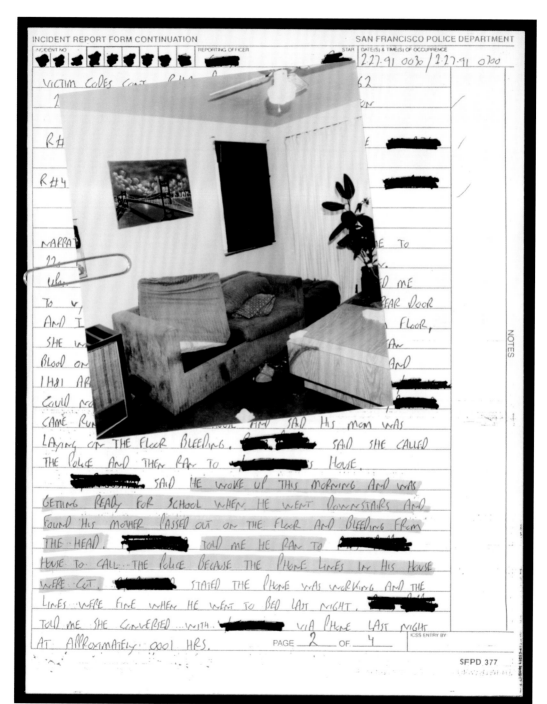

# PANDORA'S BOX

Nick Broomfield had once wanted to make a film about *Carnival Strippers*, but when I met him in the eighties there was really nothing left to film. The girl shows had effectively been closed down by protests and the economics of the expanding sex industry. Nick was then commissioned by HBO in the mid-nineties to make a film on S&M, and had already been scouting in Japan and England. When he found Pandora's Box, an S&M club on 18th Street in New York, he said it was like *Carnival Strippers* for a new decade. He invited me to come to see it.

I rode my bike to 18th Street, went up the elevator and entered. It was like a film set or the backstage of a theatre. I was stunned by the imagined landscape and the level at which the interiors had been constructed, how the walls were painted, and how each room had its own identity – The Versailles Room, The Medical Room, The Dungeon. I was fascinated by the sense of performance and the ways in which the mistresses chose their clients and the clients their mistresses. The dominatrix might select the 'punishment', but ultimately the client defined the degree to which they wanted to be whipped or what sort of equipment they wanted used. This process of choice was highly negotiated and had a transactional quality. I was again drawn to being behind the scenes, and documenting their relationships and the nature of the work.

Initially I had no idea if my pictures served any purpose. They had nothing to do with Nick's film, which he was finishing when Pandora's Box moved to another location. Even though the new space was only ten minutes away and I could work there easily, the club now seemed almost tawdry in its theatricality. I simply stopped shooting and put the work aside.

Over many years I had been hearing about forced violence and the corresponding trauma. I had heard about what happened in interrogation cells and I had seen those spaces. Ten years later we would all see what had happened in Abu Ghraib. At

Right: Entombed by Mistress Kayla, The Dungeon, Pandora's Box, New York City, 1995
Pages 230–31: Mistress Catherine after the Whipping I, The Versailles Room, Pandora's Box, New York City, 1995
Pages 232–33: Mistress Brigitte, The Dungeon, Pandora's Box, New York City, 1995

Pandora's Box I was witnessing an individual choose to participate in what looked from the outside like a violent act. But it represented play in a controlled setting where the man could say, 'Mercy, mistress', and it stopped. Still, I found that challenging. And as with *Carnival Strippers*, it was the power relations that really captured my attention – women who wield a kind of power that is suspect to others.

I knew I could go back and pursue Mistress Raven, the owner, or some of the other mistresses, and try and portray the duality of their real lives as opposed to their fantasies. I knew about the larger life they were part of and the invisible subculture that surrounded them, but I made a choice not to get lost in that world. It felt like a place I was not sure I wanted to go. Despite the sense of being on the edge, Pandora's Box was still a safe confined space and I knew the boundaries. The underground slave culture is amorphous and terrifyingly real. Its current could drag you under. There is a subtle process here: you allow yourself to immerse and then you have to pull out. It's also true in historical terms that you go down some temporal river and then you have to reach the bank, but the river flows on. Knowing when to get out takes judgment and I think it is intuitive. Sometimes you feel some sense of incompleteness as opposed to a sense of the circle or the cycle of return.

Why are circles special? We are in these *triangular* relationships, with photographers, subjects and viewers each having pointed and distinct perspectives. The circle is unifying. Everyone is equidistant from the centre. The circle is equalizing. At the heart of it is an implicit collaboration. We are all here, looking at each other.

The frontline is not just a geographical space; it is a cultural boundary, a social edge, a point of interface with time, a deep psychological frontier. The documentary photographer can cross the line and show that the conflict zone is not just a battleground in a distant land; it is also in our homes, it is self-inflicted, it is in our heads.

Right: Mistress Delilah's Tender Touch I, The Role Play Room, Pandora's Box, New York City, 1995
Pages 236–37: Bondage by Mistress Astrid II, The Dungeon, Pandora's Box, New York City, 1995
Pages 238–39: The Dungeon, Pandora's Box, New York City, 1995

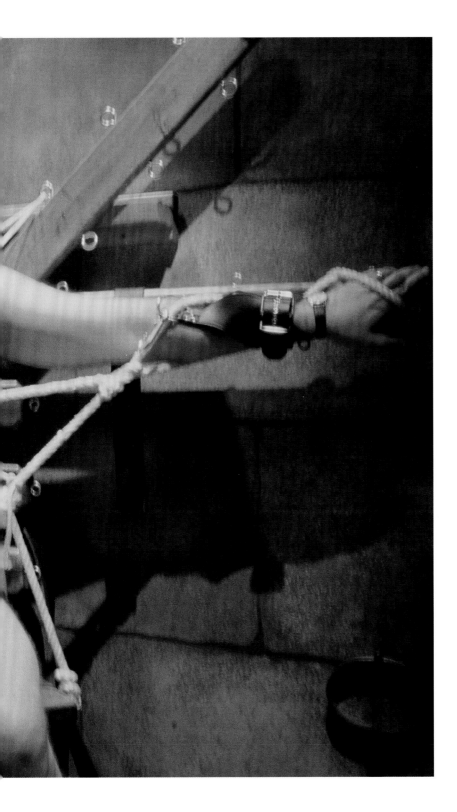

# BIOGRAPHY

Susan Meiselas was born in Baltimore, Maryland, in 1948. She received her B.A. from Sarah Lawrence College in 1970, and her Ed.M. in visual education from Harvard University the following year.

Meiselas's first major photographic essay focused on the lives of women performing striptease at New England country fairs, whom she photographed during three consecutive summers while teaching photography in New York City public schools. *Carnival Strippers* was originally published in 1976 by Farrar, Straus & Giroux. A selection of the work was installed at the Whitney Museum of American Art, New York, in June 2000, with a new edition of the book produced by Steidl/Whitney in 2003.

In 1976, Meiselas was invited to join the photographic cooperative Magnum Photos. Around the same time, she turned her attention to a group of young girls living in her neighbourhood of Little Italy, New York. The photographs made between 1976 and 1978 would become the body of work entitled *Prince Street Girls*, published later as a monograph (Yellow Magic Books, 2013). The initial photographs inspired a forty-year relationship that has been sustained to this day, despite being interrupted by work in Nicaragua and elsewhere.

Meiselas is perhaps best known for her coverage of the popular insurrection in Nicaragua and her extensive documentation of human rights issues in Latin America. In June 1978 Meiselas made her first trip to Nicaragua, and on July 30th that year one of her iconic images was published on the cover of *The New York Times Magazine*. She published her second monograph, *Nicaragua: June 1978–July 1979*, in 1981, reissued with Aperture in 2008; an edition in 2016 added an augmented reality component. Her image of Pablo Jesús Aráuz, the 'Molotov Man', made on July 16, 1979 – the eve of Somoza's departure, just before the triumph of the Sandinistas – has become an icon of the revolution. The image was revisited and re-contextualized in the installation *The Life of an Image: 'Molotov Man' 1979–2009*, which was exhibited in New York at Galerie Lelong, and was shown at Tate Modern, London, as part of the travelling group show *Conflict, Time, Photography*. The series includes a black-and-white contact sheet and duplicate slides of the moments captured before and after the iconic image, as well as the original photograph, along with examples of how the iconic image has been re-appropriated in magazines, posters and murals over time.

Meiselas served as an editor for two collaborative projects, both of which support and highlight the work of regional photographers. The first, *El Salvador: Work of Thirty Photographers* (Writers and Readers, 1983), also features her own images. The second project, *Chile from Within* (W. W. Norton, 1991), focuses on work by photographers living under the Pinochet regime. On September 11, 2013, it was released as an updated multimedia e-book in remembrance of the 40th anniversary of the Chilean coup (MAPP, 2013).

Aside from her still photographic work, Meiselas has co-directed three films: *Living at Risk: The Story of a Nicaraguan Family* (1985); *Pictures from a Revolution* (1991), with Richard P. Rogers and Alfred Guzzetti; and *Reframing History* (2004), with Alfred Guzzetti. *Pictures from a Revolution* takes Meiselas back to Nicaragua, searching for the subjects whom she photographed a decade earlier. *Reframing History* continues this exploration of a place over time, when Meiselas returns, with nineteen murals of her iconic images, to place them back in their respective landscapes within four Nicaraguan towns.

In 1992, Meiselas was named a MacArthur Fellow, a year after her first visit to Kurdistan. The five-year fellowship enabled her to produce *Kurdistan: In the Shadow of History* (Random House, 1997; University of Chicago Press, 2008). With a team of international researchers, Meiselas integrated her own photographs into a timeline of diverse image-makers, from missionaries and eccentric travellers to anthropologists and colonial administrators, juxtaposing distinct historical perspectives accented by primary materials. The result is a visual history for a country without a national archive. The book was produced along with the pioneering website *akaKurdistan* (1998), an online archive of collective memory and cultural exchange. *akaKurdistan* has been re-conceived as an artifact of this early process, currently being shown as a physical map with hanging story booklets made by contributors from the Kurdish diaspora worldwide.

Meiselas's 2001 monograph *Pandora's Box* (Trebruk/Magnum Editions), an exploration of an underground New York S&M club that began in 1995, led to the travelling exhibition *Intimate Strangers*, which compares and contrasts these sex workers with those seen in the 1970s as portrayed through *Carnival Strippers*.

The 2003 book *Encounters with the Dani* documents a sixty-year visual history of outsiders' discovery of and interactions with the Dani, an indigenous people of the highlands of West Papua, Indonesia. The work draws on a similar approach to that used in *Kurdistan*, gathering a history of multiple perspectives to create an archive of artifacts, contextualized by primary accounts. An installation of materials was featured in the first International Center of Photography triennial, *Strangers*, in 2003.

The relationship with senior curator Kristen Lubben led to Meiselas's retrospective book and exhibition *In History* (Steidl/ICP, 2008), which was produced with ICP, New York, and received the Kraszna-Krausz Photographic Book Award. *In History* not only highlights Meiselas's three seminal bodies of work, *Carnival Strippers*, *Nicaragua* and *Kurdistan*, but also questions the documentary practices used to produce the works.

Meiselas has had one-woman exhibitions in Paris, Madrid, Amsterdam, Frankfurt, London, Los Angeles, Chicago and New York, and her work is included in both American and international collections.

In 2008, Meiselas led the initiative amongst the member photographers of Magnum Photos to form the Magnum Foundation, and served as the Foundation's first acting executive director and president. A non-profit drawing on the history and values of Magnum Photos, the Foundation champions in-depth, independent documentary photography that fosters empathy and social engagement. The Foundation aims to sustain the practice of documentary photography through project support for emerging and regional photographers focused on under-reported social issues.

In May 2011, five members of Magnum Photos began the *Postcards from America* project. Each installment of the series is marked by a new group of member photographers gathering in a different location across the country to capture the nuances of modern life in America. Of the five chapters of *Postcards*, Meiselas has participated in four: the inaugural Southwest road trip; *House of Pictures* in Rochester, New York; *Swap Shop*, based in Florida surrounding the 2012 election; and most recently an extended look at Milwaukee, Wisconsin, which was installed at the Milwaukee Museum of Art in July 2014. The project is ongoing and will culminate in an extensive exhibition at Pier 24 in San Francisco.

While working on *House of Pictures*, Meiselas became interested in Hickey Freeman, a high-end men's clothing factory in the heart of Rochester. The initial work made in spring of 2012 has inspired several return trips and has taken many forms. The photographs began to call her attention to, and lead her to question, other aspects of American industry, such as: What is made in America? Who makes it? An early selection of this work was installed in a garage at the 'Look3 Festival of the Photograph', Charlottesville, Virginia, in June 2013. Entitled *160 Actions To Make A Jacket*, the show brought together Meiselas's portraits, historical images from the Hickey Freeman corporate archive, and video, as well as audio recollections gathered by Meiselas to create an immersive environment.

In 1992, Meiselas was commissioned by the Liz Claiborne Foundation with five other artists to create an ad campaign to raise public awareness about domestic violence. Initially photographing crime scenes with an investigative team, Meiselas ended up sifting through materials at the San Francisco Police Department. This research led her to create collages of police reports with the photographic evidence that accompanied them.

A commission from the UK-based non-profit arts organization Multistory in Fall 2015 gave Meiselas the opportunity to return to this subject, which she had wanted to revisit since the early 1990s.

*A Room of Their Own* is Meiselas's latest work, exploring the lives of women who are survivors of domestic abuse in the Black Country, a post-industrial region in the UK. *A Room of Their Own* is a multi-layered, visual story comprised of photographs, first-hand testimonies and original art works, created through a collaborative, participatory process between Meiselas, women living in shelters, an illustrator and a writer.

Meiselas's studio and home are based in New York. Along with engagement in her own photographic work, she has served as a consultant and curator for Open Society Foundations and the Asia Society. For six years she has taught a summer course in Human Rights and Photography at New York University, drawing on her experiences in the field. She is a former Professor Extraordinaire for the Masters of Photographic Studies programme in Leiden, Holland, where she taught for six years, after being part of the adjunct faculty at the Graduate School of Journalism at UC Berkeley. Between her various positions held in New York and ongoing travels, she continues to work on several long-term photographic projects.

# BIBLIOGRAPHY

Monographs

*Carnival Strippers* (Farrar, Straus & Giroux, 1976; revision Steidl/Whitney Museum of American Art, 2003)
*Nicaragua: June 1978–July 1979* (Pantheon, 1981; Aperture, 2008, 2016)
*Kurdistan: In the Shadow of History* (Random House, 1997; University of Chicago Press, 2008)
*Pandora's Box* (Trebruk/Magnum Editions, 2001)
*Encounters with the Dani* (Steidl/ICP, 2003)
*In History* (Steidl/ICP, 2008)
*Prince Street Girls* (Yellow Magic Books, 2013)
*My Life for Love/Nicaraguita* (Steidl/ifa, 2016)
*Prince Street Girls* (Subscription Series No. 5: TBW Books, 2016)
*A Room of Their Own* (Multistory, 2017)


Edited by Susan Meiselas

*Learn to See* (Polaroid Foundation, 1975)
*El Salvador: Work of Thirty Photographers* (Writers & Readers, 1983)
*Chile from Within* (W. W. Norton, 1991)
*Chile from Within* (e-book: MAPP, 2013)

# INDEX

Figures in **bold** refer to main entries
Figures in *italic* refer to illustrations

Amaya, Rufina 104
Amin, Bakhtiar 146, 148
Arbus, Diane 16, 26
'Archives of Abuse' **220–27**: San Francisco, California 220 ff., *221* ff.
Argentina 52, 104, 150

Barzani, Masoud 148
Bonner, Ray 104
'The Border' **120–29**: Encinitas, California *122–23*, *126–27*; Oceanside, California *124–25*, *128–29*; San Diego, California 120; Tijuana, Mexico *121*
Broomfield, Nick 228
Bush, President George H. W. 146

'Carnival Strippers' **20–33**: Boston, Massachusetts 22; Carlisle, Pennsylvania *28–29*; *Carnival Strippers* (1st pub. 1976) 22, 26, 52, 228, 234; Essex Junction, Vermont *30–31*; Fryeburg, Maine *32–33*; Tunbridge, Vermont *21*, *23*, *24–25*
Carter, President Jimmy 52
Cartier-Bresson, Henri 202
CEPA Gallery, Buffalo, New York 27

Chamorro, Pedro Joaquín 58, 63
Chantre, Ernest 150
Chile 52
Colombia 52
'Cova da Moura' **202–19**: Lisbon 202, 204, 205
*Crossings* exhibition (Chicago, 1990) 120
Cuba **52–57**: Havana *53* ff.

'The Dani' **194–201**: Baliem Valley 194, *195* ff.; Pyramid *200–1*

El Salvador 52, 61, **98–119**, 120: Aguilares 105; American churchwomen (murdered) 101, *116–17*; Arcatao *99*; Atlacatl Battalion *100*, 104; Cabañas *114–15*; Cuscatlancingo *112–13*; El Mozote (massacre) 101, 104, *118–19*; El Playon 98; San Salvador 98, 101, *110–11*; Santiago Nonualco *116–17*; Usulután 100

'44 Irving Street' **16–19**, 22: Cambridge, Massachusetts *17*, *19*
Friedlander, Lee 16

Gardner, Robert 194, *197*
Guatemala 120
Guillermoprieto, Alma 104
Guzzetti, Alfred 135

Hoagland, John 101
Honduras 61, 82, 104

Hussein, Saddam 146, 148, 150, 151, 182, *250–51*

Indonesia 194–201; *see* 'The Dani'
Iran 146, 148
Iraq 148, 182

Karlin, Marc 62
Khanum, Adela 151
Koudelka, Josef 202
Kurdistan **146–91**, 202; *see also* Northern Iraq: *Kurdistan: In the Shadow of History* (1st pub. 1997) 172, *173* ff., 182, *184–85*, *191*

Magnum Photos (agency) 60, 146, 202
Mates, Ian 101
Mexico 120, *121*; *see* 'The Border'
Mitterrand, Danielle 146, 148
'Molotov Man' *92–93*, 94, 132, *136–37*, *138–39*, *248–49*, *252–53*
Muhammad, Qazi 151
Museum of Modern Art, Lisbon 204

*New Documents* exhibition (New York, 1967) 16
*The New York Times* 60, 63, 78, 104
*The New York Times Magazine* 78
Nicaragua 52, **58–97**, 98, 105, 120, **132–45**, *248–49*, *252–53*: Estelí *76–77*, 79, 80, *84–85*, 88, *92–93*; Jinotepe *70–71*; León 83, 88; Managua 58, 61, *66*, *68–69*,

244

Pages 246–47: Downtown El Paso, Texas, 2011
Pages 248–49: Stencil mobilizing the popular militia against the Contras based on 'Molotov Man', Estelí, Nicaragua, 1984
Pages 250–51: Portrait of Saddam Hussein at military headquarters, Sulaymaniyah, Northern Iraq, April 1991
Pages 252–53: Wall previously painted with image of the 'Molotov Man', blackened before election campaign,
Masaya, Nicaragua, 1991
Pages 254–55: The north pit in Grave A, a father and son, Koreme, Northern Iraq, June 1992

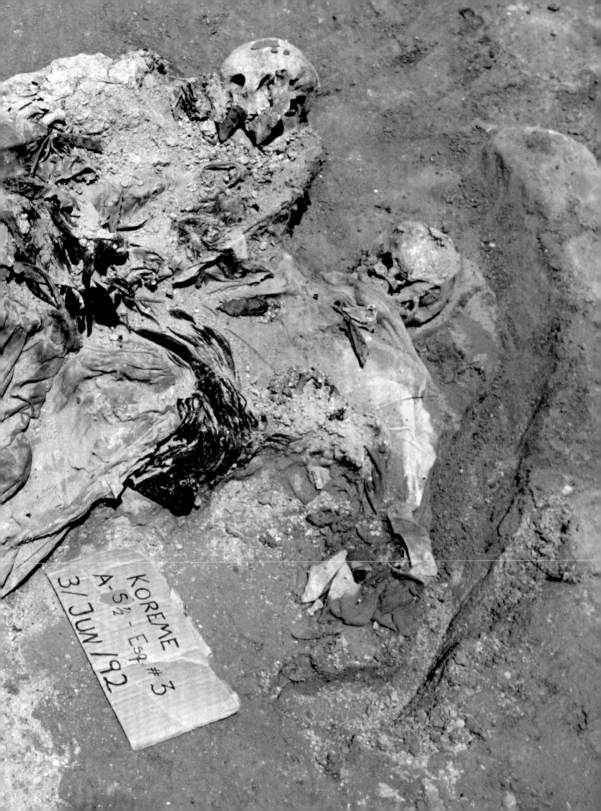

KOREME
A-5½-Es# #3
3/JUN/92

First published in the United Kingdom in 2017 by Thames & Hudson Ltd,
181A High Holborn, London WC1V 7QX

The narration starting on page 62 comes from the film *Voyages*,
produced in collaboration with director Marc Karlin in 1985 for
Channel 4, London. The text on page 96 is comprised of notes written
during the preparation of *Voyages*, 1983. All other texts are drawn from
interviews with Susan Meiselas by Mark Holborn, New York, April 2016.

Designed by Jesse Holborn, Design Holborn

Susan Meiselas Studio: Studio Manager, Alex Nelson

British Library Cataloguing-in-Publication Data
A catalogue record for this book is available from the British Library

ISBN 978-0-500-54471-6

Printed and bound in China by C&C Offset Printing Co. Ltd.

To find out about all our publications, please visit
**www.thamesandhudson.com**. There you can subscribe
to our e-newsletter, browse or download our current
catalogue, and buy any titles that are in print.